Praise for *Affirm Your Truth*

~~~~~

"You have blessed my life considerably and <u>my heart is very full. This dramatically changed the way I feel</u>, and made me feel like a success."

"<u>The peace of mind</u> in knowing I am becoming my ideal self has had a HUGE impact on my life."

"I deeply appreciate your incredible work. I'm near the end of my second round of Affirm Your Truth. I highly recommend it to others - **it has been a complete game changer for me.**"

- Brent Clayton, USA

~~~~~

"Thank you for everything! I now have the tools to keep my life truly amazing. Whenever I have off days I now go straight to these messages I have saved and it gets me back on the track of my amazing life."

"<u>I have never been so positive and content within myself and with my life</u> and it is all thanks to your fantastic work!"

"Everything is falling into place. Thank you, thank you, thank you. I couldn't be more grateful. It's been awesome."

- Rita Yost, United Kingdom

~~~~~

"My life has changed. <u>I am happier now than I have ever been</u>. I am renewing my faith in God that was lost 30 years ago. **I am positive**. I am quitting my job after 23 years to pursue a happier life. Thank you!"

- Janice Lall, United Kingdom

~~~~~

"I found your course very helpful. I'm a recovering alcoholic of nearly 23 years and this helps me take my program to a deeper level through your structure and discipline."

- Tony Williamson, United Kingdom

~~~~~

"I feel like I am becoming a more positive thinker. I feel I am starting to get control of my run away freight train mostly negative mind. I am a tough case."

- Tommy Bruce, USA

~~~~~

"I'm really pleased with Affirm Your Truth and its results."

"It's powerful enough to rewire your mind, which I did not believe. This grants freedom. My improvement has been huge, much bigger than I could expect."

"I think we all are kind of invaded by resignation. We believe that after a long time doing things in a certain way, routine is stronger than the will to change and nothing can be done to go in a different way. **But the good news is that we can reprogram our minds any time."**

"Aaron, many thanks. **For me this is now a way of life, not just a temporary action.**"

- Carles Andres Rodrigo, Spain

~~~~~

"**I have gotten more from your daily messages than I ever did in my counseling sessions.**"

- Cathy Peterson, USA

~~~~~

"The daily emails and information have enabled me to develop this habit!"

"You've helped me to get from a <u>pretty negative state to one which is so much nicer.</u> **I'm much happier & my days are brighter.**"

"I am (most of the time) feeling calmer and more focused. I'd been trying to achieve a happy state, **but had no idea how to get there**. I was always up & down fighting internally, my negative thoughts often winning out."

"**Your guidance has helped me to combat a lot of that negativity**. It is a fantastic life skill. I will continue with the daily affirmations, to continue my self development."

Tara Hayes, Australia

~~~~~

Download The Audiobook Free!

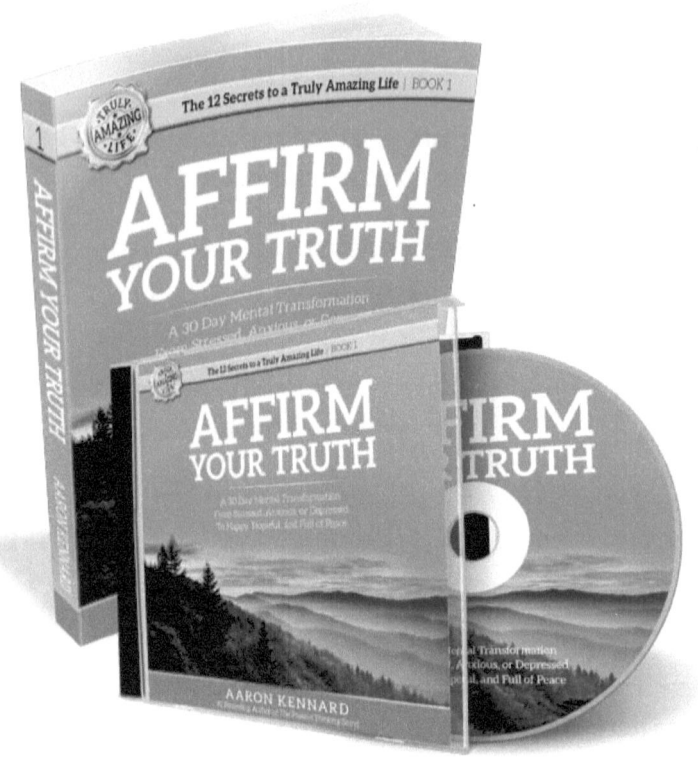

READ THIS FIRST

Just to say thank you for downloading this book, I would like to give you the audiobook MP3 version 100% FREE!

Go to http://trulyamazinglife.com/ayt-audio

AFFIRM
YOUR TRUTH

A 30-Day Mental Transformation
From Stressed, Anxious, or Depressed
To Happy, Hopeful, and Full of Peace

AARON KENNARD

Published By:
Truly Amazing Life, Inc.
4985 Moorhead Ave #3518
Boulder, CO 80305
Website: www.trulyamazinglife.com
Email: support@trulyamazinglife.com

Copyright © 2015 by Aaron Kennard

All rights reserved.

Contents

INTRODUCTION

The 'Affirm Your Truth' Promise 1

The Best Way To Read This Book 6

Additional Help & Resources 11

The 12 Secrets to a Truly Amazing Life - A Brief History 14

One More Tip and One Essential Tool 20

DAILY MESSAGES

Day 1 - Create the habit of affirming. 25

Day 2 - You become what you think about! 31

Day 3 - Be disciplined...but also be kind to yourself. .. 35

Day 4 - Time to drive these beliefs even deeper into the subconscious. 41

Day 5 - Belief releases creative POWER. It triggers the power to DO. 47

Day 6 - What is faith and why is it so important? 53

Day 8 - You are on the path. You're becoming a Jedi Master. 59

Day 9 - The simplest way to measure & improve your mental health 65

Day 10 - The nuts and bolts of habit creation. 73

Day 11 - Every adversity contains a powerful seed ... 81

Day 12 - A short personal story on the power of affirmation. 87

Day 13 - Have you been shaping your destiny lately? 93

Day 15 - Allow yourself to dream. 97

Day 16 - Does it require belief when you can see and touch it? 101

Day 17 - The power of habitual imaginations. 105

Day 18 - How to choose to be happy. 109

Day 19 - Become your own master by imprinting good images in your mind. 115

Day 20 - If you are 'staying busy' but feeling lousy, what kind of a life is that? 119

Day 22 - Achieve harmony in life through alignment. 125

Day 23 - Remember the importance of the little things. 131

Day 24 - What do you think about when you don't have to think about anything? 135

Day 25 - We are all hypnotized into NOT believing. De-hypnotize yourself! 139

Day 26 - Direct your own life using the simple science of habit 143

Day 27 - You hold the key to your destiny. 147

Day 29 - If you are doing anything and you feel bad, STOP! 153

Day 30 - Remember the importance of the 10,000 strikes. 159

CONCLUSION
So What's Next? 165
What To Expect Going Forward 172
In Closing 173
How You Can Help! 175

The 'Affirm Your Truth' Promise

These days noise and distraction bombard us from every angle. Connected more than ever as a worldwide family we have unlimited opportunity at our fingertips. But along with the abundance of options comes an abundance of confusion.

There is so much to live for, to explore, to be and to do...life can be thrilling...<u>or completely overwhelming</u>. Especially with the setbacks and obstacles that incessantly creep up year after year.

We dream.

We set a goal.

We get knocked down.

Over and over and over. We keep trying and sometimes we succeed! But often life feels draining and sometimes we find ourselves going through the motions. Responding to the daily "How are you?" with: "I'm getting by." Or, "I'm surviving."

<u>What happened to thriving!?</u>

What about the **thrill** and **joy** we once had?

It's so easy to wake up and find ourselves struggling to feel passion or enthusiasm for life and this problem is more pervasive than ever. You're not alone if you're fighting this battle.

If you ever feel worn out, discouraged, or depressed — like life has beaten you up and left you just hanging on — this book has the power to produce a profound shift in your life.

These pages contain a proven process to help you **stop suffering, find peace, and start living a *deeply happy life*** in the next 30 days or less, *no matter what* your current circumstances are...

...And it only takes about 10 minutes per day...including your time spent reading this book.

Welcome to ***Affirm Your Truth!***

You're holding in your hands a transformational habit training system that can radically shift your life from a place of stagnation, frustration, and doubt...

...To a life of **love, joy, faith,** and ***pure enthusiasm*** to just be alive today.

This is much more than a book — this is a system of daily guidance and instruction that will take you on a life-altering journey over the course of one month.

What you're about to experience has already improved hundreds of people's lives in surprisingly simple ways.

The message behind this system was first shared in my #1 Bestselling book *"The Positive Thinking Secret"* — my personal experience of discovering incredible peace, joy, and healing despite torturous pain, which was a direct result of the system you now have in your hands.

I'm honored and blessed nearly every day to hear from one of over 300,000 readers worldwide whose lives have been improved or completely transformed.

Here are just three examples of what hundreds of people have experienced with this training system:

~~~~~

"I can't thank you enough for this program! **My life has done a complete 360.**"

"At the end of last year *I was so unhappy and despondent*. Life was very challenging for me and *I had nearly lost all hope*. Each day *I just went through the motions* and *I felt numb* most of the time."

"And then you came into my life. :)"

"Your kind words and daily reminders have helped me find 'me' again! I believe in me for the first time in many years. Maybe for the first time in my life. **I now look forward to each day knowing I will enjoy it and be able to cope.**"

"Thank you for believing in me. Thank God :)"

- Glenda Woods, New Zealand

~~~~~

"Your techniques have shown me that I don't have to accept the way I feel."

"I had stuffed myself full of so much negativity that I thought feeling sad, depressed, and incapable was just a way of life, <u>now I know it's NOT!</u>"

- Leona Murdy, United Kingdom

~~~~~

"<u>It is amazing how my life has changed for the better</u> in the last 30 days because of your help."

"I now know how to live positively! <u>Nothing can stop me!</u>"

- Nate Hansford, USA

~~~~~

<u>I promise that you will experience *increased peace of mind, confidence, joy, and enthusiasm for life*</u> when you commit to following the simple daily system within these pages.

But whatever you do, don't succumb to the temptation to make this harder on yourself than it needs to be.

Don't be the person who waits until tomorrow to be happy.

Be the person who takes quick and decisive action, taking control of your life and your happiness. Be the person others look at in awe as they witness the grace and poise with which you go through life. Be the person who radiates confidence and peace because you take action without delay when it comes to your personal and spiritual nourishment.

Start right now!

You can read this intro, plus the entire first chapter, **and** take all of the actions I recommend you start with — all within the next 20 minutes.

Today is **your** day. Right now is your time to begin making dramatic changes in the way you feel about life.

I'll be here to remind you and motivate you for 6 days each week for an entire month, on one condition...

...**You just need to open the book each day and read the daily message!**

The Best Way To Read This Book

This book contains daily trainings 6 days per week for 30 days. Each day can be read in just 5 to 10 minutes and includes motivation and a reminder to take simple actions that turn into habits that will transform your life.

It's not the words in this training that will transform you — **it's your actions turned into habit that will transform your life.**

Your action is the critical factor.

This system is designed to motivate you toward simple action each and every day, long enough for a new habit to be established.

You'll get a rest day once each week so you can catch up on a day you may have missed or just focus on the simple actions we are working on. Every 7th day there is no message from me. *That is on purpose.*

There Are Two Ways To Approach This Training

I **highly** recommend the first way, but I know some eager beavers like me will opt for way #2 so I'm just going to address it here.

Way #1: Consume this book ONE CHAPTER PER DAY for the entire month and don't skip ahead.

Focus on the one brief message designed for today and then TAKE THE ACTIONS prescribed.

Way #2: Read the entire book in just a few hours. Get inspired and embed the entirety of the course into your subconscious at once.

Then go back and RE-read one chapter each day for the entire month as you TAKE THE ACTIONS prescribed.

Why do I recommend Way #1?

Because the entire key to your success with this system is to **build a habit.**

Consuming information doesn't build habits.

Reading a book will not change your habits or establish new habits. The only way to establish a habit is to **take action repeatedly** and consistently over a long period of time.

Just reading a book in a day or two will certainly inspire you — and could leave an enormous impression on you and change the way you view the world entirely.

This alone, could possibly change your beliefs enough to induce a new way of acting in the future, which could lead to transformational habit…**but it's not a sure-fire thing.**

The sure-fire, proven method of taking control and transforming your life in a systematic way — is to make a commitment to taking small, simple actions every day.

Over time these actions will form into powerful, transformative habits that work all on their own to produce amazing results in your life.

The challenge with reading the entire book all at once is that you stimulate your mind with new information, **without doing the work to apply the information.**

Our minds **crave** new information. So it's a completely natural desire for you to want to read the entire thing.

But it's MUCH more effective to give yourself little doses of 'new info' stimulation each day — and use that to motivate you to take action consistently.

When you go on an information 'binge' — it will likely lead to action for a few days or a week because you're motivated...

...But then you find yourself craving more information.

And then the information in this book is no longer 'new' so it doesn't fill that craving and you're likely to leave it on the shelf and find other 'new' information, which invites you to take completely different and unrelated action.

What's the problem with that you ask??

It seems harmless enough, you feel inspired by the other new information right? Yes, and that is fine...

...But now you are likely to forget about the action you were inspired to take last week!

And now you're off to the races applying new information, before actually acquiring a habit from the inspiring information from last week.

This is a huge challenge all of us passionate about improving ourselves face...whether we acknowledge it or not.

It's the challenge of our information age...*there's too much information and not enough consistent action!*

If we fall into this trap we risk becoming the person who is always learning yet rarely improving.

The person who knows a lot intellectually but really knows little because they have not established the habit of acting on the knowledge they have attained.

Leo Buscaglia, the amazing 'Dr. Love' was known to have said: **"To know and not to do, *is not to know*."**

So please, do yourself the service of taking this course one day at a time, and committing to yourself to take the actions I will invite you to take.

Without your personal commitment, followed up with your personal action — this system is worth probably

100 TIMES LESS to you than if you *allow it to spur you to action that creates habit*.

If you simply cannot resist the temptation to skip ahead in this book, believe me, I understand and empathize.

I don't know if I personally could resist reading ahead — I love devouring books and I often read or listen to 2 or 3 every week.

So if you're a knowledge-craving soul like me, I encourage you to hold yourself back in this case.

Let tomorrow take care of itself! Just read today's message — then TAKE TODAY'S ACTION!

The action portion of this system is probably 500 times more important than the words and instruction portion.

If you have moved on to the next day without taking the previous day's action - STOP! DO THE ACTION FIRST! Then read the next day's training.

And if you really just couldn't resist, then make sure you don't sell yourself short…keep the commitment to RE-READ each day's training when the appropriate day arrives, and take each day's action.

Additional Help & Resources

If at any time during this self-guided process you find yourself forgetting to read the daily message and feeling like you could use a bit more help or accountability...

...Here's one other option for you:

<u>I will deliver each day's message directly to your email inbox</u> at the same time each day in video, audio, and text format.

Many people have expressed that it's extremely helpful to have me showing up each morning in their email inbox to remind them and keep them on track.

To take advantage of this daily reminder system, type "http://trulyamazinglife.com/ayt-resources" into a web browser.

Because of the cost of creation, hosting, customer service, and support required to maintain that system, in the past there has been a charge for that additional level of support and help. **<u>But that is my extra gift to you for purchasing this book</u>**.

I want to make sure that I am helping you establish these habits in every possible way I can.

So I am pulling out all the stops!

Joining the daily email system is by far the most proven and effective way this system has worked for people in the past. I want you to have access to that additional tool.

But it's not required of course…you can get the exact same benefit from this program by *guiding yourself* through this book each day.

And as mentioned on the first page — you can also download the full audio mp3's of this training for free and guide yourself through the audio each day too if you prefer.

The great thing about what you've got in your hands right now is that <u>you have a permanent reference in one place</u> with all the guidance and inspiration this system provides you.

The most powerful combination is certainly using the daily email to remind you AND having the permanent record in the form of this book to refer back to.

By getting the daily email you'll be reminded to read the training each day. <u>It is so crucial that you are consistent each day</u> so that you establish a new habit.

Also, with the email you can **watch the video** and **listen to the message** from me while you read it, which engages more of your senses and emotions and drives the impact of the powerful words much deeper.

So to take advantage of the daily email method of this habit development system, type this into any web browser:

http://trulyamazinglife.com/ayt-resources

The 12 Secrets to a Truly Amazing Life - A Brief History

The course you are about to embark on for the next 30 days is part one of a 12 month training series designed to help you live the 12 Habits of a Truly Amazing Life.

Standing alone this system can be transformational. When combined with the rest of the series it has proven to be incredibly life enhancing.

Here's some background information to get you up to speed:

On the next page is the poster that started the Truly Amazing Life movement. It shows the 12 pillars, or principles, which the 12 habits are based on.

That poster was created in the spring of 2012 after months of soul searching and many hours of writing as I asked myself the question **"Why is life so amazing?"**

At the time I was experiencing what can best be described as a euphoric six month high on life. Not drug-induced, but joy-induced. Each day I was feeling completely blown away at the beauty of life, and I felt deeply compelled to capture why I was feeling such profound joy.

(Go to **http://TrulyAmazingLife.com/ayt-resources** to download and print the poster for free)

The result was that poster — which summed up the principles that were creating so much joy and making me comment consistently to myself *"This Is A Truly Amazing Life!"*

After creating that poster and seeing it so clearly, it became my mission in life to make these 12 pillars of a Truly Amazing Life accessible, attainable, and simple for anyone to live worldwide...because I felt a calling from deep within to share the experience of joy I felt & still feel in living them each day.

Over the next couple years I began to dissect those pillars and uncover the habits underneath each one. I discovered more than one habit relating to each of the 12 pillars, but I chose to focus on the one most fundamental and universal habit associated with each pillar for now...

...And that's where this book series comes in.

Over the course of about three years and thousands of hours of personal application and feedback from hundreds and hundreds of students testing these principles, a proven system and method has been created for establishing each one of the 12 fundamental habits as a permanent part of your life.

Each system is being published as a book in this series in order to allow as many people as possible worldwide to apply these transformational habits in their life.

Once the series is fully published in English, the plan is to then have it translated and published in many other languages.

These foundational 12 habits have become known as 'The 12 Habits of a Truly Amazing Life,' and they are shown on the Make Today Amazing poster here — created in 2014.

(Go to **http://TrulyAmazingLife.com/ayt-resources** to download and print the poster for free)

I encourage you to print and frame these posters and place them in your environment. It's an excellent way to help embed these essential pillars and habits into your life.

Having these posters printed will also be a wonderful visual reminder each day for you to take the actions I will be inviting you to take.

And to make it more clear, on the next page is an overview picture of the 12 Pillars, the 12 Habits, and the corresponding book related to each one:

	The Pillar	The Habit	The Book
1	Believe	Affirm	Affirm Your Truth
2	Remember	Reflect	Remember Who You Are
3	Smile	Appreciate	Feel Better Faster
4	Enjoy	Move	Move Your Body
5	Think	Meditate	Change Your Thoughts
6	Succeed	Focus	Succeed Right Now
7	Give	Serve	Give Yourself Away
8	Create	Write	Create Your Life
9	Love	Forgive	Love Unconditionally
10	Celebrate	Play	Play Every Day
11	Grow	Read	Expand Your Mind
12	Empower	Listen	Empower Other People

One More Tip and One Essential Tool

You are about to embark on the Truly Amazing Life journey by installing the affirmation habit of the first pillar — **BELIEVE**. This is the essential starting place in living a Truly Amazing Life.

Why?

Because it is through affirmation of truth that you change your deeply held inner beliefs.

Your beliefs create your automatic perceptions of the world. When you change them it is like changing the lens or filter on a camera — quite suddenly the whole picture of your life changes.

By establishing the habit of this first all-important pillar you will greatly enhance the impact and experience with all the other 11 pillars and habits.

I'm so excited for you! And I'm honored to be on this journey with you, committed to living a Truly Amazing Life.

Be patient and trust the daily process.

Start the journey today by taking the first step. Don't worry about the other 11 pillars and all that there is to learn and do.

You have all the time in the world. In fact, all you have is time, and **you are exactly where you are supposed to be right now**.

Trust that.

Whatever you experienced in the past has led you perfectly to this moment in time, which was perfectly prepared just for you to experience.

So focus on making today amazing with what you have right in front of you.

I can't wait to hear from you!

Please email me any time you feel the urge and let me know how you're progressing or tell me any challenges you are facing.

My email address is aaron@trulyamazinglife.com and I read every single email that comes through.

While I'm not able to respond personally to every email, I do respond when I can, and I definitely read them all.

I love hearing from you so don't hesitate to reach out to me.

Finally, here is an important tool I use every single day to keep me on track. It will be extremely valuable for you:

The Truly Amazing Morning Weekly Tracker

The Truly Amazing Morning™

#	The Pillar	The Habit	Mon	Tues	Wed	Thu	Fri	Sat	Sun
1.	THINK	Meditate							
2.	SMILE	Appreciate Through Deep Gratitude							
3.	BELIEVE	Affirm The Truth & Envision Your Life							
4.	REMEMBER & LOVE	Reflect Love & Forgiveness To Yourself In The Mirror							
5.	GROW	Read Uplifting, Empowering Words							
6.	CREATE	Write What Flows From Your Heart							
7.	SUCCEED	Write Your Priorities for Today							
8.	ENJOY	Move Your Body Vigorously							
9.	ENJOY	Enjoy a Healthy Breakfast							
10.	EMPOWER	Truly Listen & Genuinely Compliment Someone							
11.	GIVE	Do A Selfless Act Of Service For Someone							
12.	CELEBRATE	PLAY! (Sing, Dance, Laugh, etc.)							
	Time of Day of Self Check-in								
	How Do You FEEL? (Write 3-4 short words or statements)								

Week Ending _____

© 2014 – TrulyAmazingLife.com — Feel Free To Share With People You Love ☺

(Go to **http://TrulyAmazingLife.com/ayt-resources** to download and print the tracking sheet for free)

This tool is a weekly accountability tracking sheet containing all 12 habits of a Truly Amazing Life. I keep a stack of these printed and each week I place a fresh one at the front of my journal. I begin every day with this checklist.

It keeps me on track and helps me focus on the highest priorities first every day.

It's a guide and reminder of the specific habits of nourishing and connecting with your own soul each day.

In order to live a Truly Amazing Life you've got to **Make Today Amazing**. If you don't focus on making **today** amazing and you consistently wait until tomorrow to live fully, then you simply won't live a truly amazing life.

<u>The best way to ensure that you Make Today Amazing is by starting the day with a Truly Amazing Morning Routine.</u>

We are only focused on the 3rd habit on the list this month. But at least some of the others you are most likely already doing. Each of the other books in this series will go into great detail on the other habits...all in good time.

I encourage you to begin to implement this tool in your life.

But don't let the other 11 habits distract you from the focus on deeply establishing this one habit: **The habit to Affirm Your Truth**. That should be your highest priority for this month.

Okay, the groundwork has been laid and you now have everything you need to succeed with the pillar of 'Believe' this month.

Let's jump right in to day one and get you started on some major breakthroughs in your life!

Day 1 - Create the habit of affirming.

I'm so excited you have made the commitment to yourself to go through this *30-day transformation*.

What we're about to go through together are the ***exact things*** to do every day that are critical components for living a Truly Amazing Life.

This isn't just theory.

This is what I and many others **practice**, and the things I will share with you all contribute largely to why I am thrilled to wake up each morning and why life is an absolute joy.

For the next 30 days we are going to remain laser focused on creating the **habit of affirming the truth** that...

This Is A Truly Amazing Life

And

Everything Is Conspiring For Your Benefit

This is *by far the most important habit* you need to acquire.

It is the basis of positive thinking and a positive attitude.

It will increase your power of faith, which is the biggest source of power anywhere.

Belief is the root of faith.

Be aware that you may start to feel impatient and want to move on to creating other habits as the days progress.

Be patient. There's no rush.

There will be plenty of time to create other important habits.

And _none of them will be as effective_ if you don't first install the **habit of affirming** that everything is conspiring for your benefit.

So stick with me. **Focus** on building this one habit for an entire 30 days so that it becomes **a permanent part of you**.

Very soon you will realize you are a completely new and better person.

"By Small And Simple Things Are Great Things Brought To Pass"

It's so imperative that you *remember* and *live by* that principle.

It enables you to be patient, and know that every *small, seemingly insignificant* thing you do, is actually having a **massive impact.**

It is so easy to take small actions. But most people don't do it because they mistakenly convince themselves those small actions don't make any real difference.

FALSE!

Small things make **ALL** the difference.

A Truly Amazing Life consists of purposefully living one small moment at a time.

In fact, the only moment that even matters is this one, *right now*.

Don't be fooled into thinking small things are insignificant!

This will be simple! But not necessarily easy.

Even though what I'm going to invite you to do is **super simple,** it will require your **absolute diligence** for it to be effective.

So don't be tricked into laziness because of the easiness of the way. The smallest, simplest things in life, produce the **biggest effects**.

Here's What To Expect:

Six days per week this month there is a specially designed message prepared that will require 3-5 minutes to read.

In the daily messages I will:

- **Invite you** to take simple, specific action.

- **Remind you** in a different way each day of the habit you are building and *why it is so important.*

- **Follow up with you** to make sure you are doing the daily actions.

You may feel things get repetitive...that is on purpose!

Repetition while evoking deep emotion is a key to lasting internal change!

So stick with me for the entire 30 days.

Put your heart into *applying* what I invite you to do. I promise you will be glad you did.

Also, read this message and take the action *first thing* each day.

Don't allow yourself to be distracted by emails or anything else before you have taken the simple action I will invite you to do each day.

If you check your email first thing in the morning you are choosing to focus on other people's priorities instead of your own.

Don't Do It!

Remember this...

...**Distractions** are the **Destroyers** of your **Dreams**

Focus on *your* priority first.

Okay, time to *take action!*

Here is your #1 highest priority for the next 30 days:

Repeat these affirmations at minimum three times each day for 30 days morning, mid-day, and right before sleep:

Affirmation 1: **This Is A Truly Amazing Life**

Affirmation 2: **Everything is Conspiring For My Benefit**

That's It!!

You can absolutely do that!

But remember, don't be fooled by the simplicity and discount the importance of this priority. By small and simple things, remember?

We will add some affirmations to those as the days progress, but it's very important not to overcomplicate it.

Quality is **much** better than quantity.

And what is quality?

We'll talk about that more tomorrow.

For now just take action!

Write down those two affirmations on a note card or in your phone right now so you will have them everywhere you go.

Repeat the affirmations out loud to yourself at least three times today and first thing tomorrow morning. Then move on to the next message.

The affirmations:

- This is a Truly Amazing Life.

- Everything is conspiring for my benefit.

Take action…and make today amazing!

Day 2 - You become what you think about!

How did it go yesterday?

Did you repeat the affirmations out loud at least three times?

Did you write down the affirmations in your phone or on a card to carry them with you?

You can probably remember two affirmations easy enough, but we'll be adding more as the days go on…

…And it's helpful to see them in writing as you repeat them at least three times during the day. So make sure to write them down.

Why these specific affirmations?

'This Is A Truly Amazing Life and 'Everything Is Conspiring For My Benefit.'

The main purpose of this 30-day system is to help you acquire the habit of affirming truth to your subconscious mind. This habit is how you consciously transform your life **by transforming the beliefs** that guide your life.

You need to make it a subconscious, automatic belief that literally everything is conspiring for your benefit.

That belief needs to be such a core part of your being that it <u>automatically guides your outlook and thoughts</u>...**all the time!**

When it becomes embedded in your subconscious, you will naturally and automatically be inclined toward focusing on the positive aspect of every situation, <u>and your entire experience in life will be better.</u>

You may wonder, **"Is repeating affirmations really doing anything?"**

YES!!!

Earl Nightingale and countless others have taught:

"You become what you think about."

By consciously directing your thoughts repeatedly on something, it becomes a part of you.

And when you do that *while evoking emotion,* it becomes a part of you *much, much faster.*

So do it with FEELING!

Remember what I said yesterday:

<u>**Repetition while evoking deep emotion is a key to lasting internal change.**</u>

To enhance these affirmations, each time you repeat them, don't just say the words and move on quickly.

Stop thinking about anything else and don't rush through it.

Say the sentence out loud! It's more powerful that way than just in your head. Then pay attention to the feelings it evokes in you.

Do it with FEELING and visualization!

If you're in a quiet setting and need to whisper, like me with my kids sleeping in the rooms next to me, then whisper.

But speak the words out loud.

And the best way is to speak directly to yourself, looking in your eyes in the mirror.

Then close your eyes, repeat the words again in your head and picture at least one instance in your life that the words apply to.

Visualizing a picture in your mind internalizes the belief much faster.

For example, when I say, "Everything is conspiring for my benefit." I close my eyes and breathe deeply with a smile on my face.

Then different images come into my head.

Sometimes the image or thought of a difficult situation I was dealing with may pop in my mind.

As I picture that thing, I simply remind myself that good can be made of literally everything somehow.

I look at that thing in my mind with wonder, <u>believing that there must be something good about it</u>…even though I may not see how that's possible with how bad it seems on the surface.

And with a smile on my face <u>I *feel good* and know that all is well</u>, because everything is conspiring for my benefit.

Then I open my eyes and move on.

Simple. Quick. *But very effective and powerful* when done repeatedly every single day.

So what's your action for today?

Repeat the affirmations *with feeling* and *visualize yourself living* them three times today!

That's all for today!

<u>**Reminder of the affirmations:**</u>

'This is a Truly Amazing Life,' and 'Everything is conspiring for my benefit.'

Make today amazing!

Day 3 - Be disciplined...but also be kind to yourself.

How are you doing with the affirmations?

Are you repeating them 3 times per day?

The most common challenge I've found is *simply remembering* to do it throughout the day.

I have my affirmations printed in my 3-ring binder journal that goes with me nearly everywhere.

I also save them in a note in the Evernote app on my phone.

<u>Make sure your affirmations go with you everywhere.</u>

And until you have established the habit, some kind of reminder is essential.

You need to make a fail-proof system because you are not in the habit yet. So...

...Set a reminder!

You can set an alarm on your phone to go off at 3 different times during the day.

Or you can pick something you are already in the habit of doing at 3 different times during the day and use that as the trigger to remind you.

For example, each day you are in the habit of waking up and getting out of bed, right?

Perfect! Use that as your cue to repeat your affirmations.

Just make a decision that the first thing you will do each day when you wake up is repeat your affirmations.

It takes only a minute or so with just 2 or 3 affirmations, *including* time spent visualizing.

So obviously it's easy to do.

You just need to use discipline to do it consistently until it becomes habit.

After a while you will do it automatically without conscious thought.

Then it has become habit.

Another easy reminder is lunch and/or dinner. You can just decide that before you eat lunch each day you'll repeat the affirmations.

Then pick an evening reminder, like brushing your teeth, or laying your head on your pillow, and do it again.

Piggybacking a new habit on top of an existing habit makes it much easier to establish a new habit.

Because **in order to establish a habit you've got to be consistent**...

...And you already do your existing habits consistently! So use them to your advantage.

If you find that you're still forgetting, **use an alarm on your phone as a new cue.**

If you miss repeating them 3 times in a day *don't worry!* You haven't botched it all up and you don't need to start over.

Just continue from where you are and figure out a way to be consistent today!

You don't have to be perfect to form a new habit.

Just keep doing the small, simple thing, and if you forget once, no big deal, just start again right when you remember.

Be disciplined,...

...But also be forgiving and kind to yourself.

Recognize that anything you start new will require effort and practice and you won't do it perfectly at first.

That being said, habits are *not* formed through occasional action.

Habits are formed through consistent, repetitive action.

So don't sell yourself short by thinking that occasionally repeating these affirmations is enough.

Make it automatic and set yourself up to win! Set a reminder!

Be diligent!

This simple daily routine will absolutely transform your life.

You may not notice much change though until after you have become a new person by *religiously following the routine* for 30 days.

But as you feel good every day repeating the affirmations, that will be an immediate benefit that you experience at least three times per day.

So set your reminders and DO IT.

Your action is imperative.

Focus: Your objective today is simply to repeat the affirmations three times today with *feeling* and *visualization* – morning, mid-day, and right before sleep.

Use reminders to ensure your success!

<u>Set multiple alarms</u> on a smart phone and <u>use one of your affirmations as the title of the alarm.</u> That's one of the best ways people have found success here.

Reminder of the affirmations:

- This is a Truly Amazing Life.

- Everything is conspiring for my benefit.

Make today amazing!

Day 4 - Time to drive these beliefs even deeper into the subconscious.

How did it go yesterday?

Did you repeat the affirmations aloud, with feeling and visualization three times?

Did you write down the affirmations in your phone or on a card to carry with you?

We're going to be adding to those two affirmations today, so it's important to write them down.

And also, **did you set up three reminders so it happens by default?**

If not, stop everything and do it right now.

This message is set to self-destruct in 60 seconds and evaporate into thin air soon if you haven't done that step!

Just kidding ;)

But seriously, you need to do it!

<u>Don't rely on your memory,</u> you don't have the habit yet.

After it's a habit you can drop the reminders, not until then.

Okay, all set? Great!

Up until now we've been focused on just two affirmations to get you started right by making it super simple.

Now, if you'd like, go ahead and add in a few more.

Over the next week or so I'm going to share my personal affirmations that I have either written or gathered from various sources.

Feel free to use any of them that you want or to use them as ideas to create your own.

I place my personal affirmations in groupings as you'll see, which has helped me memorize them.

It's valuable to memorize your affirmations over time because it makes it simpler to speak them directly to yourself in the mirror...which is very powerful.

Here is the group I call 'Faith' on my personal daily affirmations sheet:

1 - With God <u>ALL</u> things are possible.

2 - All things are possible to him who believes.

3 - I help people massively increase their enjoyment of life.

4 - I free others from the bondage and suffering of their inner tyrant.

5 - <u>I walk by faith, and not by sight.</u>

6 - Faith is the substance of things hoped for, <u>the evidence of things not seen.</u>

7 - Whatever things you ask for when you pray, believe that you receive them, and you shall have them.

That's just seven, there is a bunch more and I'll share them all with you.

My habit is to repeat my big list of affirmations with feeling and visualization at least once per day.

I do it in the morning, right after I meditate, very first thing when I wake up each day.

This takes between 5 and 15 minutes, depending on how much time I spend visualizing.

I always repeat the entire list, and generally a few of the affirmations will stand out to me, so I spend more time visualizing and allowing emotions to build around those.

But in addition to my big list of affirmations, <u>I also use a short list of 5 to 10 new affirmations for key beliefs I want to install.</u>

I make a special focus of repeating this short list at least 2 to 3 times per day for 30 days, just like I'm recommending for you.

<u>This extra emphasis imprints them deeper into the subconscious.</u>

Then after about 30 days, I will pick 5 to 10 different beliefs to place my focus on.

This is a practice I intend to do throughout my life.

It is one of the most powerful and important tools I use in constantly growing and creating the life I want.

Now, let's go even deeper…

The next step for even deeper subconscious imprinting is to actually *<u>re-write each of your key affirmations</u>* <u>twice per day with a pen on paper.</u>

Don't use a computer if possible.

I recommend using any small simple notebook. Or you can write on lined paper placed in it's own separated 'tab' in a 3-ring binder.

That's how I do all my journaling now, for reasons I explain in depth in a separate book.

Any notebook or journal will suffice for this practice...so don't get hung up on that.

There is something very powerful about the act of <u>physically writing your beliefs</u>.

Getting your physical movement involved in establishing the belief creates new neural pathways in your brain faster than just speaking or thinking thoughts.

So today, grab a notebook or binder of paper and write down the 2 main affirmations as you visualize living them in your mind.

And feel free to add one or two affirmations to your routine. I'll share more of mine tomorrow.

Make Today Amazing!

Day 5 - Belief releases creative POWER. It triggers the power to DO.

Why is the habit to 'Affirm Your Truth' so important?

According to Claude Bristol who wrote *The Magic of Believing*, a fantastic and timeless book, **"It's the repetition of affirmations that leads to belief. And once that belief becomes a deep conviction, things begin to happen."**

Affirmations lead to **belief.**

Belief is the root of **faith.**

Faith is **power.**

By repeating a thought consistently for 30 days it will become *a deep conviction.*

By repeating it ***verbally*** and evoking ***deep emotion*** around the thought, ***feeling really good*** as you think it...

...it becomes a much, much deeper conviction.

And the deeper the conviction, the more **and** faster great things start to happen.

For example, in our case, *feeling amazingly stoked about life* and *thrilled out of your mind to be on this planet* :)

David J. Schwartz in **The Magic of Thinking Big**, said:

"Belief releases creative powers. Belief triggers the power to DO."

I fully agree.

Belief & faith are POWER.

Power is good! You definitely want power.

Not power over others,...

...Personal power.

Power in your self to create amazingness.

Belief triggers personal power within you.

You will only be capable of living a Truly Amazing Life in proportion to the power of the *beliefs you hold*, which determine the *thoughts you habitually think*.

The challenge is, we are ALL hypnotized into thinking negatively.

And don't think that you are somehow exempt.

We don't even notice all the ways we are hypnotized. Even though I do have a deep conviction that everything is conspiring for my benefit,

I still have certain beliefs that I'm not even aware of that are limiting my power.

So I continue to do what I'm telling you to do. Every single day I spend time updating the programming of my mind.

In his amazing book **Pyscho-cybernetics**, Maxwell Maltz teaches that we are all hypnotized to some extent.

We get hypnotized by ideas we accept from others uncritically, or by ideas that we repeat to ourselves and convince ourselves are true.

And these negative ideas have the same effect on our actions as the ideas a professional hypnotist places in the mind of their subject.

I'm sure you're aware that people will do all sorts of crazy, laughable things when they are hypnotized, that they wouldn't dream of doing in a conscious state.

<u>But the truth is we are all living our life to some degree hypnotized and controlled by beliefs</u> that we probably don't even know are controlling us!

But here's the beautiful point that Maxwell Maltz emphasizes:

"Within you right now is the power to do things you never dreamed possible. **This power becomes available to you just as soon as you can change your beliefs.**"

"Just as quickly as you can de-hypnotize yourself from the ideas of 'I can't,' 'I'm not worthy,' 'I don't deserve it,' and other self-limiting ideas."

We must de-hypnotize ourselves!

No one else will do it for us.

It's so important to acknowledge the amazing power you have within you to change your course by changing your beliefs!

Do you see how negative thought habits could be holding you apart from the Truly Amazing Life you desire and deserve?

<u>Do the small and simple thing and repeat your affirmations three times today!</u>

That is how you de-hypnotize yourself.

Don't worry about doing it perfectly.

JUST DO IT!

Keep up the diligence!

Write your affirmations with a pen at least twice daily.

Speak them into the mirror.

Feel them and visualize yourself living them!

Here are more of my personal affirmations...

...The 'Feeling' Group:

1 - Today is going to be a great day!

2 - I absolutely LOVE LIFE and I help everyone I touch love life.

3 - I'm energized! I'm enthusiastic! I'm stoked about life!

4 - I feel fantastic!

5 - I'm feeling wonderful!

6 - I CAN'T WAIT to see what amazing things God has in store for me today.

7 - I've got an amazing feeling about today.

8 - I feel happy, joyful, peaceful, and restful.

9 - I feel strong, confident, and powerful.

10 - I feel well rested, and energized, and renewed, and refreshed.

11 - I feel positive and optimistic.

That's all for today...

...Make today amazing!

Day 6 - What is faith and why is it so important?

You have now done five days of consistent affirmations...great job!!

You are well on your way to gaining **deep convictions** that will improve your life in amazing ways.

Feel free to add a few more affirmations to your daily short list now.

But keep it between 5 to 10 maximum, for the list you repeat three 3 times per day!

It's great to start building a big list of affirmations, and I highly recommend that...

...but stick with a short list this month that you are committed each day to **re-writing by hand twice** and **repeating at least thrice!** ;)

I can't emphasize enough not to try to overdo it right away.

Trying to do too much will likely backfire on you by causing you to not spend sufficient energy **visualizing** and **feeling** yourself living your affirmations.

Be patient!

It's much better to have just a few affirmations and say them with all your heart and soul consistently than to just rattle off 50 affirmations just to check it off your list.

OK, now that I've laid a sufficient beat down on that drum, here are some more of my personal affirmations that you are free to use or get ideas from...

The 'Who I Am' group:

1 - I have what it takes to do BIG THINGS that make a difference in this world.

2 - Nothing can stop me and nothing can get me down.

3 - I am a warrior.

4 - I am a finisher.

5 - I am an overcomer.

6 - I am an achiever.

7 - I am a success.

8 - I am a winner.

9 - I am a child of God.

10 - I am forgiven.

11 - I am loved.

12 - I completely and totally forgive myself and all others for mistakes of the past.

13 - I always keep the child in me alive.

14 - I am unique in all the world.

15 - I always feel good about myself because I am God's child - <u>totally forgiven and totally loved.</u>

Now here's the critical question for you to consider today…

What is faith and why is it so important?

Various people have explained it many ways over the course of human existence.

We'll discuss this from various angles this month, but here is one very practical definition proposed by the seminal author and teacher Napoleon Hill:

"<u>Faith is definiteness of purpose backed by belief</u> in the attainment of the object of that purpose."

Huh…is it really that simple?

Just have a 'definite major purpose' and convince yourself somehow to a belief that you can attain that purpose?

Well...frankly, yes. It is that simple.

But simple isn't the same as easy.

And why is it so important to develop faith?

Faith gives you the power to achieve what you want.

We want to live a Truly Amazing Life.

That is a great purpose to be definite about.

And it definitely beats the "I just want to be comfortable on as little effort as possible," mediocre, **non-purpose-driven approach** to life that afflicts so many of us at times.

That is why we are being clear with ourselves every day that **everything is conspiring for our benefit.**

We need that deep conviction because it will guide our perceptions and all of our actions.

Remember what Napoleon Hill said: Definiteness of purpose, backed by BELIEF, equals FAITH!

And faith is power.

So what do you need to do?

Be *definite* and *clear* in your purpose.

And get yourself to believe you can achieve your purpose by literally brainwashing your own **subconscious** mind through your **conscious** direction of your thoughts on a regular basis...i.e. **affirmations**.

Is it more clear now why affirmations are such a powerful tool in your life?

I hope so!

Now, let's talk about tomorrow. There will not be a message from me tomorrow. This is by design.

I highly recommend the practice of resting one day per week from the normal work and busy-ness that consumes most other days.

This practice is taught in many spiritual texts and religions, and mental and spiritual rejuvenation are the extremely nice practical benefits to the practice.

So you will notice me follow that in all my trainings by giving you one day completely off each week.

<u>I do encourage you to continue your routine of repeating affirmations though.</u>

Keep it up...you can do it! **You are well on your way to transformational habit creation.**

More on faith in 2 days...Make Today Amazing!

Day 8 - You are on the path. You're becoming a Jedi Master.

Welcome to week two of **Affirm Your Truth**. Great job taking action and sticking with me so far!

Before we press forward on our journey let's check in with 'reality' just for a moment.

If you are a human, which I can assume is the case, you have likely found yourself NOT wanting to repeat your affirmations some mornings and some nights.

I totally get that!

I've been there.

But that is when you MOST need to do it!

What I've found is that when I don't feel good, I definitely do not naturally want to repeat a positive belief. It feels hypocritical or false or weird or something along those lines.

When you notice that happen, **which it will**, that is your cue to get out a pen and some paper and write what you feel.

Be open and honest. Let your true feelings out. Don't hide from the fact that you don't feel good.

Ask yourself in writing, "Why do I feel this way?"

It is very therapeutic and beneficial. It will help you see why you don't feel good.

Then it is time to forgive yourself and everyone else so you can move on and feel better.

Look in the mirror and tell yourself these exact words:

"I'm sorry. Please forgive me. Thank you. I love you."

Those may very well be the four most powerful sentences ever strung together to release you from negativity and free you to feeling good again.

So if you ever feel bad, just try this:

1. 1. Write your feelings down.
1. 2. Look in the mirror and say. "I'm sorry. Please forgive me. Thank you. I love you."
1. 3. Think those same things toward anyone else whom you may be feeling negative toward.
1. 4. Then repeat your affirmations.

That process has helped me many times to get out of a funk, take control of my emotions, and start feeling really good again. Try it out!

Now let's talk more about...

...**What is faith and why is it so important?**

Here's another explanation of faith by Napoleon Hill in his wonderful book *Outwitting The Devil*:

"Faith is a state of mind wherein one recognizes and uses the power of positive thought as a medium by which one contacts and draws upon the store of infinite intelligence at will."

Wha? Huh? Can you repeat that?

OK, sure :)

"Faith is a state of mind wherein <u>one recognizes and uses the power of positive thought</u> as a medium by which one <u>contacts and draws upon the store of infinite intelligence</u> at will."

Clear and definite purpose mixed with belief is the essence of positive thought.

By using that 'medium' you put yourself into the state of mind where you can draw upon the store of infinite intelligence at will.

And that store of infinite intelligence is certainly stocked full of power.

Now, here is my favorite definition of Faith. It may be the most commonly known, but perhaps least understood...

"Faith is the <u>**substance of things hoped for**</u>, the <u>**evidence of things unseen**</u>." - Hebrews 11:1, (The New Testament)

Faith is literally the **actual substance** of the thing you hope for AND **the evidence** of that thing.

Think about it...if you are clear on what you want, and you believe deeply it is yours, you have faith.

And so <u>the simple act of getting yourself to believe, has actually become the evidence</u> that the thing you do not yet see exists!

Your belief is the evidence that you will have it!

Beautiful.

The key then is to keep that belief. <u>The challenge most of us have is we start doubting, and stop believing.</u>

That is why daily affirmations are so vital!

The habit to Affirm Your Truth gradually but firmly establishes deeply held beliefs that become subconscious and automatic.

<u>So how does this help you live a Truly Amazing Life?</u>

You already have a bunch of deeply held beliefs that are subconscious and automatic that are giving you your current experience in life.

What we're doing now together is upgrading your operating system with new and *better* subconscious beliefs,...

...Which will make you automatically experience a new and better life.

And even if you're already pretty positive and happy, wouldn't you like more happiness, fulfillment, and joy?

Of course you would!

So go forth young padawan!

Do your daily training.

Be diligent.

Do not be slothful because of the simpleness of the way.

You will be a Jedi Master in due time ;)

But don't be like Luke Skywalker and rush off to fight Darth Vader before you're ready.

<u>Keep doing this small daily routine with **vigilance.**</u>

It takes time.

You cannot rush the process...shortcuts simply won't work.

You are planting seeds. All seeds require a season of growth before fruit can be harvested.

Repeat your affirmations again today with feeling and visualization.

Make today amazing!

Day 9 - The simplest way to measure & improve your mental health.

You are amazing! Remember that.

It is one of the most important things to remember.

Have you told yourself that lately in the mirror? I highly recommend you do.

I'm proud of you and excited for you that you are sticking with me and taking this daily action *in faith*, believing it will work goodness in your life.

Keep it up.

Envision how quickly 30 days have passed in the blink of an eye and how you are now a new person because you diligently stuck with this small and simple daily action.

Now, here's an important question for you...

How is your mental health?

Seriously...how **mentally healthy** are you?

Before you jump quickly to an answer...consider this:

"The measure of mental health is the disposition to find good everywhere." - Ralph Waldo Emerson

There is good to be found or created in literally everything.

In the medical and psychiatric industry there are elaborate tests to 'measure' one's mental health.

But I've never heard anyone other than Ralph Waldo explain measuring mental health in such a simple way...

...And I agree with Ralph!!

I know he's right, because in 2011, <u>life became truly amazing for me as my disposition made a massive switch to seeing amazing goodness in **everything**</u>.

My turning point happened in the realization of the beauty of a sore throat, which is most often seen as a nuisance at best, but which I realized I could turn into a trigger to remind me to express gratitude.

I suddenly saw the painful nuisance as a tremendous blessing...

...And according to Emerson, that is very good mental health.

How about you?

Is it automatic for you to see the good in every single thing?

If not, it soon will be as you stay diligent!

You absolutely can become an inherently positive thinker!

And there is massive power and joy in that way of being.

If it already is automatic for you to see the good in everything, keep doing those affirmations…

…It will become an *even deeper part of you*, and make life that much better still.

There is good in literally everything…

…But what do you *automatically* look for and see?

One of the main questions I get when people are struggling to believe 'everything is conspiring for my benefit,' is along these lines:

"How would you find positivity in violent crimes and terrorism and such?"

This is a big discussion but the simple answer is explained by Maxwell Malts in another insightful section in his book *Psycho-cybernetics*.

"Much of what we call evil is due entirely to the way men take the phenomenon…"

"Since you make them evil or good by your own thoughts about them, **it is the ruling of your thoughts which proves to be your principal concern.**" - Maxwell Maltz, Psycho-cybernetics

The fact is you cannot control what others do and there will continue to be violence, crime, hatred, and 'evil' in the world.

But who decides how you react to it? Who controls what you think about it and what you DO about it?

Is there good to be found or created or done even when heinous and evil things have happened?

Always.

And the only truly rational thing a good person can do is to focus the attention on finding and making good in the situation...whatever it is.

To dwell on the negative is to give it power to consume and overrun life.

Your principal concern is the *ruling of your thoughts*!

Have you ever considered whether you might be making the facts evil or good by your own thoughts about them?

The stoic philosopher Epictetus said: "Men are disturbed not by things that happen, but by their opinion of the things that happen."

What we are working on together, is changing the way we **automatically** see the world and everything that happens. **We are changing our habitual opinions**.

And those changes are made by 'small means, in many instances.'

So continue doing the small, simple affirmations today!

Here is another group of my personal daily affirmations for you to consider for ideas of your own…

The 'What I do' group:

1 - I expect the very best today, and with God's help, I will obtain the best.

2 - Life is truly amazing and it's always getting better.

3 - Every day in every way I am getting better, stronger, wiser, healthier, and freer.

4 - I am a faithful, wise, and prudent steward over all the resources I have been entrusted with.

5 - I am an amazing financial manager. I clearly see the details of all my income and expenses.

6 - I am smart, disciplined, and faithful to myself.

7 - I spend the precious life energy of money wisely and judiciously, not frivolously.

8 - I am an over-the-top outstanding and loving husband. I constantly shower my beautiful bride Nan with love, affection, service, and romance.

9 - My wife is my queen. I adore her with ALL my heart. Bringing her joy is my highest priority and calling in life.

10 - I am an amazing father to my children. I spend quality time daily with them, teaching and playing with them.

11 - I wake up early each day to exercise my body, mind, and spirit through study, meditation, prayer, and exercise.

Feel free to use any of those verbatim or use them as ideas to write your own personalized truths! It's important to build your master document of truths to affirm.

Keep it up, you're doing great!

Keep **visualizing** and **feeling** your daily affirmations!

Everything really is conspiring for your benefit.

This really is a Truly Amazing Life, and you have the power to create your destiny.

You are driving the ship of your thoughts. You are a free agent unto yourself.

Look for the amazing today!

You will find it.

Make today amazing!

Day 10 - The nuts and bolts of habit creation.

It's time to talk a bit about **the science** behind habit creation.

A deeper understanding of how habits work will help as you continue to develop habits throughout your life.

Charles Duhigg wrote a brilliant book compiling his research on the subject called **The Power Of Habit**.

He clarifies and greatly simplifies the understanding of **how habits work,** as well as the easiest way to change them.

Every habit — whether it's a belief, a thought you think, or a physical routine — contains these 3 elements: Cue, routine, and reward.

Whenever you think a habitual thought, it's because something has given you a **cue** or a 'signal' to think that type of thought.

Then you think the thought, that is the **routine**, and then you get some type of personal **reward** or perceived benefit out of it.

Here's a visual of **the three components he asserts are present with ALL habits:**

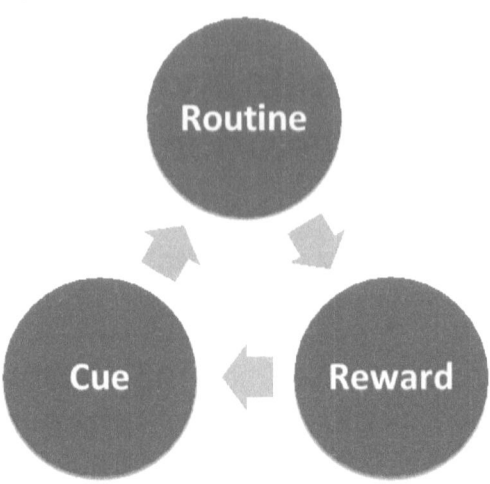

For example, imagine you stub your toe on a chair when you walk past your table one morning in your rush to grab your shoes quickly and not be late for an appointment...

...And perhaps you automatically think, "Ow! This is going to be a bad day, I can already tell!"

Then you slide on your shoes, grab your keys, and rush out the door, slamming it behind you...

...brooding about what excuse you can come up with for being late while underneath that brooding, **likely without your awareness**, you're saying to yourself...

"Why am I so clumsy when I'm rushed? I hate being late, why can't my kids just get ready when I tell them to? It's so irritating!"

What was the **routine** in this scenario?

You immediately declared the day as 'bad' which triggered a cascade of other negative self-defeating thoughts.

Routines are easy to see if you look. Just quickly scan through the previous few day's memories for any behavior you tend to repeat frequently — those are your routines.

So what was the **cue** in the scenario?

You stubbed your toe?

Perhaps.

Or maybe it was the way your children didn't behave as you would like?

And what was the **reward** in this scenario?

That one can be tricky to pinpoint.

In this case, the reward seems to be some satisfactory emotion you get out of slamming the door, and fuming and venting to yourself.

Perhaps expressing your anger or frustration is a way to 'get even' with your family for 'making your life so hard.'

Interestingly, negative thoughts can be their own reward!

Every thought we think, negative or positive, invites other similar thoughts.

So any negative thought we entertain immediately starts inviting over all its relatives and soon we're host of a full-fledged internal pity party with barely a moment's notice!

This pity party is the perfect venue for consoling ourselves as a poor victim of life.

Being consoled as a victim is **highly gratifying** to that ego part of us that doesn't want to accept responsibility for our life.

Hosting our own pity party is a very common reward with negative thinking

It may be strange to think of that as a reward, but...

...We get some kind of reward out of everything we do or think habitually...otherwise we wouldn't do it!

And that is a brief overview of how all habits work.

I share that so you can start to pay attention to the **cues**, **routines**, and **rewards** we are purposely establishing together right now.

Every day we have set up a **cue**, or reminder: Alarms on the phone, getting out of bed, brushing teeth, or heading to lunch or dinner, etc.

That cue triggers our **routine:** At least three different times we visualize and feel ourselves living our affirmations.

And our **reward?** *In this case there are multiple:*

1 - We feel better!

2 - We feel happier because we are thinking about what we want.

3 - We feel a sense of accomplishment because we know we are doing something that is greatly benefiting us.

The more rewards to a routine the merrier!

When you experience multiple positive rewards from a routine, it is a lot more likely to be a routine that you will stick with.

So make sure you are experiencing the reward *right in the moment.*

Don't just repeat the affirmation with the plan and hope of getting the reward of an amazing, fulfilled life, off in some future non-existent day once you have repeated that positive thing enough times.

Habits don't become sticky habits with contrived futuristic rewards.

<u>Habits have immediate rewards.</u> So make sure that each time you visualize your affirmations you are experiencing the reward...so the habit sticks.

<u>Make that your goal!</u> Sit with it and visualize your 3 to 5 affirmations until you literally start feeling good while you think about them.

If you struggle to feel good when visualizing your affirmations one day, don't worry. Maybe your mind is too preoccupied or worried about something.

That should be a **cue** to you for a different habit you can create: **Stop and write honestly whatever is on your mind.**

That's what I do habitually whenever I can't seem to feel good by simply re-directing my thoughts.

But I digress...we will get more into the habit of writing in the training system for the pillar of 'Create'. For now, I'll leave you today with the rest of my personal affirmations to consider...

The 'Core Beliefs' Group:

1 - Whatever I can conceive and believe, I can achieve.

2 - Everything is conspiring for my benefit.

3 - All things work together for good to them that love God.

4 - There is no bad day.

The '12 Pillars of a Truly Amazing Life' Group:

1 - I <u>Believe</u> this is a Truly Amazing Life.

2 - I <u>Celebrate</u> Life, play daily, and bring others joy.

3 - I <u>Enjoy</u> every moment.

4 - I <u>Smile</u> because it feels good.

5 - I <u>Think</u> faithfully.

6 - I <u>Create</u> art in all I do.

7 - I <u>Succeed</u> every moment of the day.

8 - I <u>Remember</u> who I am.

9 - I <u>Empower</u> other people.

10 - I <u>Give</u> myself away freely.

11 - I <u>Grow</u> every day.

12 - I <u>Love</u> unconditionally.

Make today amazing!

Day 11 - Every adversity contains a powerful seed.

A couple days ago I asked, "**What do you automatically see?**"

Today let's talk more about, "**How to create new automatic responses.**"

Do pianists '*decide*' which keys to play as the music flows from their fingertips in a concert?

Do dancers '*decide*' where to move their feet or hands or hips next while performing?

Of course not...the reaction is automatic. There is no conscious thought in the process.

We all have similar automatic reactions in our thinking. We think thousands of things without consciously '*deciding*' to think them.

And this happens all the time.

It's critical to understand, that just like the pianist and dancer formed automatic habits of beauty and grace through repeated practice over time,...

...We too will create automatic thinking habits that lead to beauty and graceful poise in the way we naturally live our daily lives.

All of our thought habits can be changed by making a conscious decision and then by 'practicing' the new thoughts consistently over time.

So keep repeating those affirmations.

Affirmation is your practice.

You want to make this automatic, and you will, very soon.

This truth spoken by Napoleon Hill should totally excite you about this affirmation practice: "Any idea, plan, or purpose may be placed in the mind through repetition of thought."

He was speaking here of the **subconscious** mind, where things become an automatic part of us.

You can create *anything* you want through repeated affirmation.

If you want a thing enough that you are willing to commit to dwelling on the thought of it repeatedly over a long period of time...eventually it will be. Because the thought will become a burning desire and focused passion in your life.

Your committed repetition installs the thought as a deeply held belief — and combined with clarity of purpose that equals *faith*.

And you now know, **faith is the power to create anything.**

By the way, Napoleon Hill studied the minds of thousands of successes and failures for most of his adult life. He was not just speaking off the cuff.

***Repetition of thought* is the key.**

Here's my all-time favorite statement made by Napoleon Hill:

"Every adversity, every failure, every heartache carries with it the seed of an equal or greater benefit."

Literally everything has potential goodness.

He repeated this in various ways throughout his works, and it is such a hope-giving belief to espouse.

Incorporating this belief in my life is largely what led me to believing firmly that…

…Everything is conspiring for my benefit.

Another influential statement of truth that deepened this belief for me was stated in the ***New Testament*** in Romans 8:28:

"And we know that **all things work together for good to them that love God**, to them who are the called according to his purpose."

Certainly we could all use "everything conspiring" for our benefit.

But is that automatically happening for everyone? I think that's a deeper question than 5 minutes allows.

If we have desires to do good in any form, I believe the source of all goodness fully supports us in that endeavor.

I doubt that we have such support if our motive is to harm or injury.

But it has been proven that even the most evil and heinous actions of humans carry a seed of benefit. Quite often they are turned to great advantage with amazing amounts of good being done in the aftermath.

Knowing that doesn't suddenly make the evil act good.

But consider the horrific evil performed by Hitler for example: My life has been forever altered for good by one of Hitler's captives Victor Frankl.

Frankl survived and used the experience to inspire me and millions of others — showing us how to find meaning and joy in life regardless of our circumstances, by using our agency to direct our own thoughts to gratitude and meaning.

Read his amazing book, **Man's Search For Meaning**, for more incredible insight on this topic.

But what about that, **"To those who are called according to his purpose,"** part of the statement in Romans 8?

Well, what person who has desires to do good is not called from God according to his purpose?

Is that desire from within not a calling from your soul? From your true nature? From the spirit of God within you?

If anyone has desire to do good, that desire must be a calling from God, because, "all things which are good cometh of God." - Moroni 7:12 (The Book of Mormon)

So remember...

You absolutely can create new automatic thought responses and ways of seeing *everything*.

You do it through repetition of thought...i.e. affirmation.

Remember...

Every adversity carries the seed of an equal or greater advantage.

Remember...

All things work together for your good.

Remember...

Everything is conspiring for your benefit!

And keep reminding yourself those things with feeling!

Repetition combined with emotion is how you convince your subconscious...

...And that changes everything.

Make today amazing!

Day 12 - A short personal story on the power of affirmation.

If you have gotten the feeling by now that I'm passionate about re-programming the mind, your feelings are definitely on the right track! ;)

And there's a reason.

I am consistently amazed and blown away time and time again as I look back at the results in my life that I can directly attribute to **systematically** changing my thought habits.

Here's just one striking personal example...

In the early days of starting my real estate investment business I needed to secure quite a lot of investment capital in order to buy, renovate, and sell houses. But after over a year I had only come up with about $500,000.

I needed $2 Million or more for my business to survive and thrive.

So on the advice of my insightful mentors, I wrote this affirmation and began repeating it multiple times every single day, visualizing myself living it:

"*I have over 2 Million dollars of investment capital at my fingertips.*"

Every day I **religiously** repeated that and clarified the picture of myself in my mind using that investment capital in my business.

But for nearly two months I struggled. I felt like I kept slamming into brick walls — blocked at every turn...mostly from within my own mind, which came up with every excuse in the book for not putting in the work required.

Then my coach pointed out an error in my *thinking*.

He helped me see that I was afraid of rejection, and that the fear was destroying all my efforts.

In order to overcome the fear he essentially **commanded** me to go and get 50 people to tell me "NO," and to **not stop** until I had accomplished that objective.

"Hmmm...kind of an odd objective," I thought, since I need people to tell me 'Yes' if I'm going ever accomplish the ultimate goal!

But I trusted him, and continued repeating the affirmation and visualizing it. But I also began immediately to require myself to ask at least five people *per day* to loan me money and get them to tell me "No".

Well, I failed miserably at my new goal.

I simply couldn't do it.

The problem was… <u>nearly everyone I asked told me "Yes!"</u>

Within the next 30 days I had over $2 Million in committed funds, and I have never lacked for investment capital since.

I still don't think I have reached 50 'No's' eight years later.

What's the point?

Clear affirmations of what you desire to **have** or **be** or **do**, repeated daily, with feeling and visualization… <u>work for anything and everything</u>.

I would not have taken the proper actions in the right way if I had not been visualizing my desired outcome every single day with feeling.

The constant affirmation produced the *energy*, *resilience*, and *clarity of purpose* required.

In your case, I'm guessing there is likely **at least one major thing** or attribute that you would love to have, be, or do that has been eluding you.

If you want it badly enough, then do this:

1 - <u>Write a short sentence describing exactly what your life would look like if you had that thing or attribute already.</u>

You've got to paint the picture of the end result so you can easily visualize it.

2 - <u>Then add that affirmation to your short list of 5 to 10 affirmations.</u> Visualize and feel it three times minimum every single day.

And don't stop after just one month if it hasn't fully transpired. Some big things may take months or even years of focus.

<u>A word of caution:</u> Don't overwhelm yourself with a **huge list** of affirmations for your short list. Don't try to change a bunch of things about your life all at once.

That will likely backfire because it's too difficult to be consistent when you try to do too much and <u>you may never get the habit.</u>

Be patient.

Keep it simple!

Focus on the few things most important to you.

It's wonderful to keep a big list of affirmations you repeat once a day...

...But keep your **most important affirmations** to a list of just 5 to 10 so you get in the habit of focusing a lot of energy on them daily.

Have a wonderful day!

Make today amazing. :)

Day 13 - Have you been shaping your destiny lately?

"Man is the **master of thought**, the **molder of character**, and the **maker and shaper** of condition, environment, and destiny." - James Allen, *As A Man Thinketh*

You shape your own destiny

So, how about it? <u>Have you been shaping your destiny lately</u>?

Yes, you have!

Whether you have realized it or not, everything you have ever thought or done has shaped your destiny.

The key to shaping and creating an *amazing destiny* is to <u>**be deliberate about everything you think.**</u>

Of course, that's not as easy as it sounds.

Hence this training system!

As you establish this habit of repeating affirmations with feeling and visualization every day, **you are becoming a more deliberate thinker daily.**

This will empower you to expand your life and increase your joy in amazing ways.

James Allen also had this to say on the topic: "Your **vision** is the promise of what you shall one day be; your **ideal** is the prophecy of what you shall at last unveil."

Do you have a **vision**?

What is your **ideal**?

If our vision is the promise of what we shall one day be, and our ideal is a prophecy, then let's make sure we focus on a vision and ideal we actually want!

Can you tell me right now, without a second thought, what the vision and ideal for your life are?

OK, I'll give you a few seconds to just think about that answer.

What is your vision and ideal for your life?

What destiny do you want to create?

Hopefully some or all of the affirmations you have been repeating came to the forefront of your attention.

It's okay if not, that will come in time.

But hopefully it's clear to you now how repeating affirmations that reflect your ideal and a vision of what you desire is highly beneficial.

The affirmations I have shared with you are my ideal and my vision of a Truly Amazing Life.

Holding them high in my mind continues to fulfill their prophecy daily in my life.

It will do the same for you.

As you constantly hold a vision of a Truly Amazing Life in your mind, that becomes the only possibility for what you can have.

That's all for today...go have some fun!

Tomorrow there's no message from me.   Take a day of rest!

- Rejuvenate.

- Be with family and friends.

- Serve people selflessly.

- Take a complete break from all your work.

Regardless of how much you think you have to do, you will be glad you took a break!

But keep on **visualizing your key affirmations** and **feeling amazing**.

Make today amazing!

Day 15 - Allow yourself to dream.

Welcome to week three in your thought transformation!

Today I want you to just picture yourself in your mind living this way for a moment:

Slow down for a minute and picture yourself...

Celebrating life, playing daily, and bringing others joy.

Enjoying every single moment.

Smiling constantly.

Automatically *thinking* faithfully.

Creating art, beauty, and the life you want.

Succeeding every single day.

Remembering who you are.

Empowering others.

Giving yourself away freely.

Growing every day, leaving your comfort zone often.

Loving everything and everyone unconditionally.

Can you feel how a life lived that way is a Truly Amazing Life?

Do you want to live a Truly Amazing Life?

Of course you do!

So keep holding that vision in your mind.

Play the movie of that vision daily by **saying** those words, **seeing** yourself living that way in your mind, and **feeling** how amazing it feels.

"As a being of power, intelligence, and love, and the lord of his own thoughts, man holds the key to every situation, and contains within himself that transforming and generative agency by which he may make himself what he wills." - James Allen (As A Man Thinketh)

You hold the key to your own destiny.

Don't hold yourself back!

You really do hold the key. There are no limits to what you can become.

Don't settle for mediocre!

Hold your worthy ideal high in your mind, today, and every day.

Those affirmations are a very high and worthy ideal, and any other worthy ideals you add to that are wonderful.

And don't be afraid to dream BIG!

"Dream lofty dreams, and as you dream, so shall you become." - James Allen

But remember, a dream for just one day dies.

Dream your dream daily and it ***must*** come to pass.

It's so easy to get distracted, to lose sight of our dreams, and to slip back into complacency in life. That's why this habit of daily affirming your truth is so powerful and so important. It gets you back on track daily.

Your task is simple vigilance to daily focused thought. This keeps your dreams alive and visions alive.

More tomorrow…

…Make today amazing!

Day 16 - Does it require belief when you can see and touch it?

Great job sticking with me!

You are well on your way to new powerful thought habits now.

Keep it up! You can do this for 30 days and it will absolutely improve your life.

If you have slipped at all from being vigilant about your affirmations three times per day, <u>**don't start worrying about it.**</u>

Just make it your mission again today to do that one simple thing three times.

<u>**Don't think** about tomorrow or yesterday...they are **completely irrelevant.**</u>

Just **focus** on your next simple action and **do it**.

Okay, let's check in with the amazingly influential Abraham Lincoln to kick off our morning right...

"To believe in the things you can see and touch is no belief at all; <u>but to believe in the unseen is a triumph and a blessing.</u>" - Abraham Lincoln

Belief itself is a victory! Think about it...

It's not easy to believe in the unseen!

It takes work, practice, dedication, discipline, and diligence.

Most people won't do it.

Fortunately you are not like most people! You wouldn't have started this program let alone made it this far if you were.

Fulfillment and power come by growing our 'believing muscles' throughout our entire lives.

Would you agree, now that you are over two weeks in, that it takes discipline to create a new habit?

<u>Keep being disciplined,</u> you will absolutely love yourself for it. <u>Being master of yourself feels amazing.</u>

"The world in which you live is not primarily determined by outward conditions and circumstances **<u>but by thoughts that habitually occupy your mind.</u>**" - Norman Vincent Peale, **The Power of Positive Thinking**

I absolutely love Norman Vincent Peale.

He is one of the most inspiring people I have ever encountered...I hope I can give him a big hug someday.

He dedicated his life to improving ours.

I <u>highly recommend</u> you read everything he wrote. And it's so important to let this truth he shared sink in deeply...

...Your world is primarily created by your thought habits!

Certainly we all want to live in a beautiful, abundant, amazing world.

So...just get *beautiful*, *abundant*, and *amazing* thoughts to habitually occupy your mind!!

<u>Pretty simple right?</u>

Just keep on affirming those beautiful, abundant and amazing thoughts! Every day you are strengthening the habit.

And that is how you create for yourself a beautiful world to live in.

Many may think it's just in our perception...that changing our thoughts about something doesn't change the thing. <u>But that's simply not true</u>.

It is true that our thoughts shape our perceptions...

...And it's also true that our perceptions shape our reality, and have a major impact on our circumstances.

Don't let up now, this is the time to remain diligent!

Hopefully you have found yourself in a good routine by now...it will likely be feeling pretty natural and habitual now in this third week of effort...**but don't take your foot off the pedal yet!**

Keep the diligence up all the way through the entire month...you need to make sure you crest the hill so you can enjoy the long ride as the newly created habit pulls you along in amazing ways in the future.

More tomorrow...

...Make today amazing!

Day 17 - The power of habitual imaginations.

Continuing from yesterday's conversation regarding habitual thoughts, here Norman Vincent Peale says it in a slightly different way:

"There is a deep tendency in human nature to become *precisely* like that which you habitually imagine yourself to be."

You become your habitual imaginations.

So, how do you "habitually imagine yourself to be"?

Do you habitually imagine at all?

Yes! You definitely do.

You imagine all the time automatically. Most people don't even realize what they imagine, and life is a mystery.

The wise person purposely directs their imaginations.

You are removing the mystery by creating your own habits of thinking and imagining a worthy ideal. So cultivate your habitual imaginations each day as you are affirming your truth.

Remember...

To believe is a triumph!

You are achieving the greatest possible success in life by directing your beliefs.

Remember...

You are what you habitually think.

How can you predict your future?

You are *creating* your desired future world by creating your thought habits.

At this stage many people may find themselves slipping into the rut of routine while repeating affirmations.

You DO want an automatic routine, but...

...You DO NOT want a rote, empty routine devoid of positive emotion.

So keep striving daily to put your entire heart into this routine each time.

Your goal every single time you repeat your affirmations is to...

...**GET EMOTIONAL!**

Feel *different* and *better* every single time. Don't just repeat and move on. <u>*Do whatever it takes to get emotional*</u>! This is vitally important!

You are not repeating affirmations every day just to have another task on your list to check off.

You are doing it with the intention of evoking amazing feeling emotions.

You are not primarily doing this to create a better future. The future doesn't exist and you can never possibly experience the future. Only *right now* exists. The only experience you will ever have is *right now*.

You are repeating these positive, uplifting affirmations to create an amazing feeling reality right now — this very day.

Don't allow yourself to fall into a rut of unconscious routine and let life slip by you. That is missing the entire point of life: **joy.**

<u>There is no joy in unconsciousness.</u>

Let the routine serve you by helping you stay fully **aware**, fully **awake**, and fully **involved** in every moment.

Feel better right now! That should always be your primary objective.

And you will feel better through conscious affirmation of your truth. Good thought produces good feeling. Good feeling is positive energy vibration. It puts you into a state of joy. Living in joy is the whole point.

And as a wonderful side effect — feeling good and living in joy ends up putting you on a path that leads to all sorts of beautiful, surprising, and further awe-inspiring circumstances.

It's a virtuous cycle.

Stay awake today. **Feel *everything***.

Make today amazing!

Day 18 - How to choose to be happy.

"The mental vision which you create and firmly hold in consciousness will be actualized *if you continually affirm it in your thoughts* and *if you work diligently and effectively.*" - Norman Vincent Peale

So...how do you to turn your vision to reality?

Just two steps...

Step 1: Continually affirm your vision in your thoughts.

Continual, persistent affirmation turns your vision to reality.

Check.

We're doing that.

As the days and months go just continue to add to your vision.

Step 2: Work diligently and effectively.

The key to working diligently and effectively is to get yourself feeling amazing emotionally.

The level of emotion you put into your affirmations will determine the level of energy your beliefs provide you.

<u>This energy will be your source of your power.</u> You need energy first and foremost in order to be capable of working diligently and effectively.

If you try to **force yourself** to work toward your visions you won't be able to sustain the effort required.

But each time you evoke positive emotions while thinking on your visions, you receive energy and power from within. It is often surprising how quickly energy can come, seemingly out of nowhere, when you focus your thoughts clearly on what you want, with belief.

<u>This energy is what enables you to work diligently and love it.</u>

Now let's see what else Norman had to say…

"When you get up in the morning, you have two choices — either to be happy or to be unhappy. <u>Just choose to be happy.</u>" **-** Norman Vincent Peale

Happiness really is a choice

But how do you 'just choose to be happy'?

<u>By consciously choosing happy thoughts.</u>

That's all.

What are happy thoughts?

Thoughts that make you feel happy ;)

More specifically, **thinking about what you want** and **believing you will get it**.

If you think about something you want, and you don't believe you can get it, you feel bad.

Doubt and disbelief are not happy thoughts.

Your disbelief actually means you are thinking of *not* getting what you want, or the lack of it.

So choosing happy thoughts requires belief…which is the entire point of this 30-day system!

We are strengthening our 'believing muscles' through affirming our truth, which increase our belief that we actually can get what we truly want…

…Which at the root for all of us is **JOY**.

And along those lines, if you believe you won't get what you want (which feels bad),…

…Then you are actually praying for, and asking for, whatever you don't want.

Just another reason why believing is so critical.

You do receive whatever you believe.

Your feelings will show you your beliefs...whether you are doubtful or faithful. Good feelings equal belief. Bad feelings equal doubt.

Pay attention to your feelings!

"And all things, whatsoever ye shall ask in prayer, believing, ye shall receive them." - Matthew 21:22

As you continually repeat affirmations of what you want, if you feel bad, that means you don't believe you can have or be those things.

And you won't get them or become them living in that state. Not to mention that state of feeling bad is opposite of experiencing joy right now in life.

That's why it is so critical that you *get emotional* and *feel good*.

Your feelings are your indicators of belief.

Remember,...

...Persistent affirmation turns your visions to reality.

Remember,...

...**Happiness is a choice.**

Remember,...

...You receive what you believe!

Remember to…

…Use your feelings as your guide.

And finally…

…Three times today, get yourself worked up emotionally, ***feeling good*** as you repeat and visualize your affirmations.

If for some reason you repeat the affirmations and you don't feel good, you may want to write the question, "Why don't I feel good?" in your journal and then dump out your true feelings on paper.

That often opens the floodgates and frees you up to start feeling better.

Make today amazing!

Day 19 - Become your own master by imprinting good images in your mind.

How did you feel yesterday?

Did you get emotional?

Getting yourself worked up with positive emotion is awesome. Not only is it the way to increase belief, but also it immediately increases your quality of life!

If you feel amazing right now, isn't that all you truly want in life anyway?

Say yes!

Belief is power.

Faith is power.

"We walk by faith, not by sight." - 2 Corinthians 5:7, *The New Testament*

This is a great affirmation to add to your list if you were to add one. It is definitely on my list:

<u>I walk by Faith, not by sight.</u>

It is a very good thing to convince yourself that faith is how you live your life.

But let's talk more about your vision. The amazing author and coach Bob Proctor said, "<u>You must be able to see yourself, with your inner eye, already in possession of the good you desire.</u>"

First you must see it clearly in your mind.

Each day as you affirm and visualize, you will clarify your vision of yourself already having and being what you desire.

We become what we see inside.

Maxwell Maltz confirms this also. In ***Psycho-cybernetics*** he said: "**Our self image, strongly held, essentially determines what we become.**"

Maxwell's story is fascinating.

He was a plastic surgeon, who realized that many of his clients could not actually benefit from feeling better about themselves using plastic surgery, because as long as their self-image didn't change, nothing could help them.

Some people he treated had success with plastic surgery, because changing what they saw in the mirror actually enabled them to change their self-image.

But for the majority it didn't work that way.

This led him to completely change fields altogether and focus on helping people change their inner self-image rather than just transforming their outer image.

He did amazing work and through his books continues to help many people change their inner-image and totally enhance their quality and enjoyment of life.

<u>What we are working on is purposely changing our own self-image.</u>

That is why we are repeating powerful, lofty ideals of ourselves, multiple times per day with feeling.

W. Clement Stone said something really important on this: "**Self-suggestion makes you master of yourself.**"

You master yourself **by** creating your own self-image.

You create your own self-image through 'self-suggestion.'

Self-suggestion = <u>Affirmation</u>

So…

<u>**Affirmations make you master of yourself!**</u>

BE a master of yourself.

Affirm your truth <u>with all your heart.</u>

As you can tell, I'm going to keep hammering this point every day for 30 days…you will thank me for it later! Or quite possibly you're already thanking me for it…I have received dozens and dozens of emails of gratitude for this transformative help from people who have only been one week into the process.

I wish someone had helped me focus on this simple practice 10 or 20 years ago.

But I'm grateful to know now…and I'll keep affirming my truth daily. How about you? Keep it up!

You are awesome. You can do it.

Make Today Amazing!

Day 20 - If you are 'staying busy' but feeling lousy, what kind of a life is that?

Do you feel totally in the groove of this habit yet?

Are you getting value and benefit by *feeling really good* each time you repeat your affirmations?

GOOD! *That is the ideal.*

It isn't just future value we're working on here, though that is one of the perks.

Our primary concern is to feel amazing right now!

That is at the core of living a Truly Amazing Life.

And affirming your truth with heart, you should be feeling really good at least three times each day.

This is training you to pay attention to your feelings and make living in a good feeling state your #1 priority.

Feeling good is extremely important.

If you don't feel good 2 problems occur:

1. 1. You don't feel good ;)
2. 2. Things don't tend to work out that great…you experience resistance!

<u>That's a bad combo!</u>

If you do feel good, that's a good enough reward in itself. But then as a bonus, **everything just seems to flow and work out so much nicer!**

Or at least you roll with whatever happens in a peaceful state rather than getting agitated,…

…Which allows you to abide in the faithful state of knowing and actually believing that *everything is conspiring for your benefit.*

<u>Your first priority before anything else is to *feel good*.</u>

I never like to work on anything if I'm not feeling good. Usually I just stop what I'm doing, and figure out how to feel better first. It's often counterproductive to attempt to do things when you don't feel good.

On the other hand, sometimes just taking action does get you feeling better.

But be careful with this one. It's really easy to just 'stay busy'.

But what kind of life is that?

If you are 'staying busy' doing stuff while at the same time feeling 'off' or 'frazzled' or 'unsettled,' you're not living in a state of joy.

Better to stop and address your emotional state!

You will know right away whether the action you are taking invigorates you and makes you feel better or whether it's just masking an emotional pain or unsettled feeling.

If you feel worse with action, **STOP**!

Do something to get yourself feeling better.

(And that generally doesn't mean go and eat something. That is often counterproductive. Ask me how I know.)

Oh...you want ideas? Okay, try on any one of these 3 for starters:

1 - Pull out your journal and write.

2 - Shut off all potential distractions, close your eyes, and breathe in and out slowly for five minutes, letting go of each thought as it passes through your mind.

3 - Get outside and walk or jog around. Drop to the ground and do 50 pushups. Do a bunch of jumping jacks! Whatever works for you! Often the most important thing you can do to feel better is to move your body vigorously.

I do all of those every single day as part of my morning routine — in addition to visioning and affirmations and other things.

It's all part of nurturing the mind, body, and spirit in order to feel centered, invigorated, connected and in love with my own self. Loving yourself and truly nurturing your body or soul will get you feeling better fast!

BUT BEWARE: The easiest, most natural thing to do when we are feeling bad is to sabotage ourselves.

The body often craves sweet food, or distraction of the mind. Those things do provide some immediate comfort and trick us into thinking we feel better — but usually they just leave us feeling worse!

Whereas doing something truly nurturing for your self has only positive consequences.

So if you feel bad today and find it difficult to feel it repeating your affirmations...

...Take action to get yourself feeling better first! It's so important.

Then *Affirm Your Truth* again!

By now at the end of 3 weeks of work, you likely already have a new habit. We're in the final strengthening phase now.

We'll take a day of rest from the daily training messages tomorrow. <u>But keep on affirming your truth.</u>

Make today amazing!

Day 22 - Achieve harmony in life through alignment.

Napoleon Hill once said: "One must marry one's feelings to one's beliefs and ideas. That is probably the only way to achieve a measure of harmony in one's life."

So get your feelings hitched to your beliefs!

But how do you marry your feelings to your beliefs and ideas if you don't acknowledge and give attention to your feelings?

As you are well aware, I suggest paying close attention to your feelings...and get yourself feeling really good.

If you feel good, that means you're thinking about what you want...you are thinking faithfully and you are full of belief.

If you feel bad, look at what you're thinking!

You are absolutely thinking along the lines of **doubt**, **fear**, or **worry** about something. Those are the opposite of belief.

If you feel bad, that is your indicator that you are not thinking faithfully.

Faith and belief always feel good.

When you notice you feel bad, change your thoughts.

As you know, affirmations are a great way to do that.

Rhonda Byrne in her fantastic book **The Secret** said, "Ask once, believe you have received, and all you have to do to receive is feel good. If you are feeling good, it is because you are thinking good thoughts."

You can tell if you believe by how you feel.

Rhonda Byrne also said, "Everything you see and experience in this world is *effect*, and that includes your feelings. The cause is always your thoughts."

When I finally grasped that concept — that I could always control my feelings by changing my thoughts — it changed my entire experience in life.

What does life consist of if not our feelings?

Isn't how you feel all that really matters at the end of the day?

Or the start of the day?

Or at any point in the day?

Living the 12 pillars of a Truly Amazing Life makes you feel good.

If you go through life feeling amazing consistently isn't that a Truly Amazing Life?

That is why these 12 pillars are so vital:

That's why they are **the pillars** of a Truly Amazing Life...

...They hold everything up.

Those are the thoughts to think that make you feel great. And they lead to actions that help you feel fantastic. It's a wonderful cycle, test it out!

I'm sure you have.

But go ahead and think and do any one of the 12 pillars and I guarantee you will feel better.

And that's why I created this poster showing **The 12 Habits of a Truly Amazing Life:**

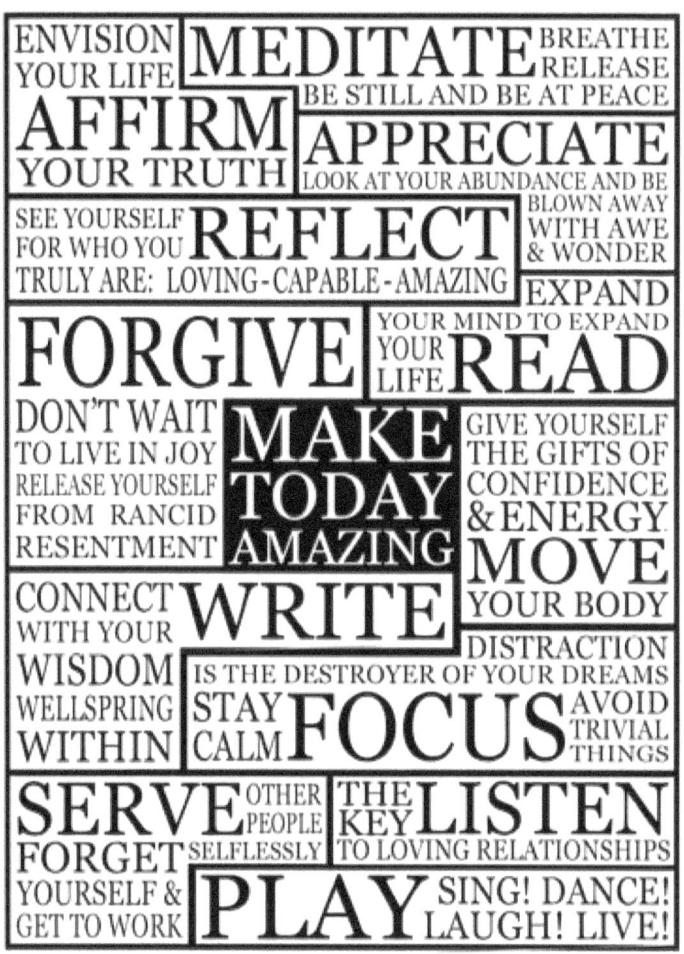

(Go to **http://TrulyAmazingLife.com/ayt-resources** to download and print the posters for free)

I have posted these two posters throughout my home, because they remind me constantly, both consciously

<u>and subconsciously, to think of the things that make me feel good.</u>

They remind me that life is truly amazing, and they remind me of the specific things I can think and do to Make Today Amazing.

You can see the resources page above for links to all the other versions and sizes of those posters in case you want something a little bigger or more permanent than you can print from your computer.

Keeping these reminders in front of you and in your environment will help more than you can even quantify…because it works on a subconscious level just being in your field of perception.

Keep it up. **_Affirm Your Truth!_**

Make today amazing!

Day 23 - Remember the importance of the little things.

Congratulations on passing the three-week mark of affirming your truth!

We are in the homestretch now. You likely already have a permanent habit, but let's not take any chances. Keep up the diligent effort for this final week and let's seal the deal.

It's only one more week...such a small amount of time.

But it is making a HUGE difference.

Remember...

..."**By small and simple things are great things brought to pass**; and small means in many instances doth confound the wise." - Alma 36:6, *The Book of Mormon*

For context, this statement was made by a man named Alma to his son Helaman.

He had told his son of the immense importance of the small act of cleaning the metal plates that their records were inscribed upon, so that they could be of value to future generations.

If they weren't cleaned regularly, the plates would tarnish and degrade, and the record would become illegible, losing all its value.

If they were cleaned diligently however, they would be of great value to future people.

Now we see an actual example of that principle bearing out, since so many lives have been touched and improved as a result of that small, simple act of cleaning those records.

<u>What we are doing together this month is a very small and simple thing.</u>

It's not a big hard task to get these two truths imprinted in your subconscious mind:

- **This is a Truly Amazing Life**

- **Everything Is Conspiring For Your Benefit**

This only takes a few minutes per day of consistently directing your thoughts.

<u>But it's a small and simple thing that will **massively enhance** the quality of your experience in life.</u>

"**A wise man will be master of his mind. A fool will be its slave.**" - Publilius Syrus

So Be Wise...

...Like our buddy Publilius suggests.

Who is this Publilius guy you ask?

He was a Syrian slave in Italy in the first century BC who won his own freedom from his physical master by his own wit.

Then he wrote tons of smart stuff in Latin...so we should pay attention. Anyone who's writing smart maxims in Latin must be someone worth listening to!

Just kidding...kind of.

But that was a pretty profound statement by Publilius!

And knowing he was literally a slave owned by another man definitely gives the statement more potency.

He knew as well as anyone that **sometimes you cannot control your outer circumstances.**

When he said, "A wise man will be master of his mind. A fool will be its slave," he was presenting the most fundamental choice any of us can make in this life:

Will we master our thoughts or be controlled by them?

Nobody outside of us has the power to force us to keep thinking a certain way. That is the one domain where no matter the circumstances, nobody can remove from us our individual freedom to choose our thoughts.

We alone hold the power to either master our mind or be a slave to it. We make that choice each day by how we decide to direct our thoughts.

Which thoughts will we allow ourselves to entertain?

Which thoughts will we reject?

Which thoughts will we consciously repeat over and over in order to imprint them on our subconscious mind?

All of these things decide our freedom. The wise person doesn't leave it to chance.

So I applaud you for your wisdom in doing the simple daily practice and mastering your mind.

Keep it up! With every single increase in mental mastery, **no matter how slight**, your life becomes another notch more amazing.

So keep going!

Make today amazing!

Day 24 - What do you think about when you don't have to think about anything?

We are on the homestretch of a powerful month of habit creation.

Now it is time to review where we have been, and re-emphasize the most important points we have covered together.

Doing this each day for our remaining days together will go a long way to solidifying these beliefs and locking them firmly in place in your subconscious mind. Stick with me this final week and you'll be very glad you did!

So here we go...

Day 1:

This is the most important habit of all the 12 habits of a Truly Amazing Life: **Affirm Your Truth.**

It is the key to the critical pillar of BELIEVING that, **'This Is A Truly Amazing Life'** and **'Everything Is Conspiring For Your Benefit'**.

This is the basis of positive thinking and a positive attitude.

Belief is the root of faith...and *faith is power*

"By small and simple things are great things brought to pass."

Small things make a MASSIVE difference.

Distractions are the destroyers of your dreams.

Day 2:

"You become what you think about." - Earl Nightingale

Be aware of what you are thinking about and be intentional in your thoughts **all the time.**

Since you become what you think about, remember to ask yourself, "What am I thinking about? What am I becoming?"

Are you filling your mind with things you want to become?

This is the crucial question to consider:

What do you think about when you don't have to think about anything?

Do you turn first to filling your mind with the latest of other people's Twitter or Facebook posts?

Or do you default to checking your email or the latest news?

I'm not suggesting any of those sources of information are inherently detrimental, but I do think it's worth paying attention to how you feel and asking the question, **"Am I thinking about what I want to become?"**

<u>Day 3:</u>

Make sure your short list of affirmations is going with you everywhere! Carry a notebook, or write them in a note-taking app in your phone.

Set a reminder!

You need either an alarm set on your phone, or a daily routine which you can add the affirmation routine to.

<u>Are your reminders working for you?</u>

If not, it's never too late to adjust them and try something else. Be open to finding the thing that works great for you!

<u>Day 4:</u>

It's good to start building your BIG list of truths to affirm.

Repeating some or all of them daily at least once is a great thing to do throughout life, **in addition** to your focused effort on your key 5 to 10 affirmations short list.

Feel free to use my list of affirmations, change it, expand on it, whatever you want.

You can download my entire list of affirmations on the 'Affirm Your Truth Resources Page' at http://trulyamazinglife.com/ayt-resources.

And finally...**write your key affirmations daily at least once.**

There is something very powerful about the act of physically writing your beliefs.

Keep on affirming your truth!

Make today amazing!

Day 25 - We are all hypnotized into NOT believing. De-hypnotize yourself!

Let's continue our review of the powerful principles of **creating the habit to *Affirm Your Truth!***

Day 5:

"It's the repetition of affirmations that leads to belief. And once that belief becomes a deep conviction, things begin to happen." - Claude Bristol

"Belief releases creative powers. Belief triggers the power to DO." - David J. Schwartz

Belief and faith are POWER.

Power is very good.

But we are ALL hypnotized into not believing, or in other words, doubting and thinking negatively.

"Within you right now is the power to do things you never dreamed possible. **This power becomes available to you just as soon as you can change your beliefs.**"

"Just as quickly as you can de-hypnotize yourself from the ideas of 'I can't,' 'I'm not worthy,' 'I don't deserve it,' and other self-limiting ideas." - Maxwell Maltz

We must de-hypnotize ourselves!

But how do we do it? How do we root out the automatic hypnosis our underlying beliefs have subjected us to?

Do the small and simple thing and repeat your affirmations three times today!

That is how you de-hypnotize yourself. Through consistent repetition with feeling you can replace the subconscious beliefs driving you.

Day 6:

What is faith and why is it so important?

"Faith is definiteness of purpose backed by belief in the attainment of the object of that purpose." - Napoleon Hill

Just get clear on your 'definite major purpose' and persuade yourself to believe that you can attain that purpose!

That is faith. Faith is power.

Day 8:

"Faith is the substance of things hoped for, the evidence of things unseen." - Hebrews 11:1

Your belief is the actual evidence that you will have what you want!

If you ever feel bad, and don't feel like repeating your positive, life giving affirmations...do the following:

1. **Write your feelings down on paper**. Be real with yourself. Get your true thoughts out of your head no matter what they are.

2. Look in the mirror and say: **"I'm sorry. Please forgive me. Thank you. I love you."**

3. Think those same 4 sentences toward anyone else you may feel negative toward, or whom you simply feel you may have let down. Allow yourself to get emotional. Tears are a good thing.

4. Then repeat your positive life giving affirmations.

<u>*You will almost certainly feel much better after that 4-step process.*</u>

That process has helped me get out of a funk, take control of my emotions, and start feeling really good again more times than I can count.

Try it out!

Day 9:

You are amazing!

Remember that. It is one of the most important things to remember.

Tell yourself that every single day in the mirror. <u>It's so important you remember to love and appreciate yourself.</u>

"The measure of mental health is the disposition to find good everywhere." - Ralph Waldo Emerson

<u>How healthy are you?</u>

Is it becoming more and more automatic to see the good in every single thing?

Remember what Epictetus said: "Men are disturbed not by things that happen, but by **their opinion of the things that happen.**"

That's why we are conditioning ourselves to look for the good in everything. Then we will live a hopeful, optimistic, undisturbed and joy filled life.

We are mentally healthy and we live a vibrant life.

<u>Affirm Your Truth</u> in order to nurture your mental health.

Make today amazing!

Day 26 - Direct your own life using the simple science of habit

Let's continue to reinforce our habit of believing through our review and the power of repetition...

Day 10:

Remember the science behind habit creation?

Every habit — whether it's a belief, a thought you think, or a physical routine — contains these 3 elements: Cue, Routine, and Reward.

It's a great idea at this point to review the cues, routines, and rewards you have set up regarding your habit to Affirm Your Truth.

<u>Is the process working?</u>

Can you identify the cues, routine, and rewards?

The cue for your daily affirmation habit is the reminder or alarm you have chosen to use that will happen like clockwork three times per day.

The Routine is the action of looking in the mirror and repeating, or just speaking out loud, or writing your key 5 to 10 affirmations.

The Reward is feeling good! And the satisfaction of knowing you are becoming a more powerful master of your mind with every small and simple act of good feeling repetition.

Day 11:

Remember what Maxwell Maltz said: "What we need to understand is that these habits, unlike addictions, can be modified, changed, or reversed, simply by taking the trouble to make a conscious decision — and then by practicing or 'acting out' the new response or behavior."

We can and will create new automatic thought patterns and habits, which change our entire experience in life.

And this applies to *anything*.

As Napoleon Hill reminds us, "Any idea, plan, or purpose may be placed in the mind through repetition of thought."

And then there's my all-time favorite statement made by Napoleon Hill:

"Every adversity, every failure, every heartache carries with it the seed of an equal or greater benefit."

That statement was highly influential on creating the statement **'Everything Is Conspiring For Your Benefit.'**

Which was also influenced largely by the powerful statement in Romans 8:28: "<u>And we know that all things work together for good to them that love God.</u>"

Day 12:

Remember my experience with raising investment capital? It was the repeated affirmation that broke through the mental barriers holding me back from my goal.

<u>You can apply this habit to Affirm Your Truth to literally have, be, or do whatever you strongly desire in life.</u>

You get to decide much of what is true for you. Create your vision and your ideal. Believe it is possible. This becomes your truth. Then simply *Affirm Your Truth* and watch it materialize in your life.

Day 13:

"Man is the master of thought, the molder of character, and the maker and shaper of condition, environment, and destiny." - James Allen

<u>Like it or not you have been **constantly** shaping your destiny.</u>

Now you are **consciously shaping** your destiny more and more, and leaving less to the chance of **subconscious shaping**.

Remember…

…"Your vision is the promise of what you shall one day be; your ideal is the prophecy of what you shall at last unveil." - James Allen

See your ideal vision and continually affirm it so you don't unconsciously revert to a vision you don't want.

Make today amazing!

Day 27 - You hold the key to your destiny.

We're nearing the end of our 30 day journey of mental mastery...don't stop now! Let's finish strong!

Day 15:

"As a being of **power**, **intelligence**, and **love**, and the lord of his own thoughts, man holds the key to every situation, and contains within himself that transforming and generative agency by which he may make himself what he wills." - James Allen

Don't hold yourself back!

Don't settle for mediocre!

Hold your worthy ideal high in your mind.

"Dream lofty dreams, and as you dream, so shall you become." - James Allen

Don't be afraid to dream BIG!

And be vigilant at dreaming daily so your dreams don't die.

Day 16:

"To believe in the things you can see and touch is no belief at all; <u>but to believe in the unseen is a triumph and a blessing.</u>" - Abraham Lincoln

Keep up this daily discipline of growing our 'believing muscles' and you will triumph at winning the life you want.

"The world in which you live is not primarily determined by outward conditions and circumstances <u>but by thoughts that habitually occupy your mind</u>." - Norman Vincent Peale

Your world is created by your thought habits

Your job is to create truly amazing thought habits so that you live a Truly Amazing Life!

Day 17:

"There is a deep tendency in human nature to become precisely like that which you habitually imagine yourself to be." - Norman Vincent Peale

You become your habitual imaginations.

So how do you "habitually imagine yourself to be"?

Remember, avoid doing your affirmations just to check them off your list!

You DON'T want a rote, empty routine *devoid of positive emotion.* That's missing the point.

Your goal every single time you repeat your affirmations is to **GET EMOTIONAL!**

Feel *different* and *better* every single time.

Let the routine serve you by helping you stay fully **aware**, fully **awake**, and fully **involved** in every moment.

Feel better right now!

That should always be your primary objective.

Day 18:

"The mental vision which you create and firmly hold in consciousness will be actualized *if you continually affirm it in your thoughts* and *if you work diligently and effectively.*" - Norman Vincent Peale

Continual, persistent affirmation turns your vision to reality.

I can't over-emphasize that the key to having the energy to work diligently and effectively is to get yourself feeling amazing emotionally.

Feeling good should be your top priority.

It's a worthy goal you can strive for your entire life.

And you can succeed at it every day. Earl Nightingale defined success in this most empowering way I have ever heard: "*Success is the progressive realization of a worthy goal.*"

So...*succeed right now* — by doing something to get yourself feeling better.

And remember what Norman Vincent Peale said: "When you get up in the morning, you have two choices - either to be happy or to be unhappy. **Just choose to be happy.**"

Happiness really is a choice.

But it's a choice that often requires ACTION.

So choose to be happy today and then DO something about it.

If you notice yourself feeling bad, first change your thinking! Don't mask your feelings and hide from it. Then take some action to move your body, write, meditate, breathe, or serve someone and you will absolutely start to feel better.

Take a break tomorrow!

Give yourself the gift of disconnection...it is such a valuable gift.

Love your self and your work enough to leave it alone for one day. It will expand your creative mind and fill you with energy.

Now go have some fun and *Make Today Amazing*!

Day 29 - If you are doing anything and you feel bad, STOP!

Today is our final day of review and the 2nd to last day in our 30-day mental mastery transformation. Let's jump right in...

Day 19:

Are you getting emotional?

Getting yourself worked up with positive emotion is instantly life altering and highly beneficial.

Not only is it the way to increase belief, but also it immediately increases your quality of life!

As you get yourself feeling loving energy, it makes it easier to live this affirmation: **I walk by *faith*, not by sight.**

As you **Affirm Your Truth**, and you see yourself in your mind living your ideal, you will feel better. That is how you walk by faith...

...You see the future in your mind and you feel good because you believe it.

It's really that simple.

First you must see it clearly in your mind.

Maxwell Maltz confirmed this in **Psycho-cybernetics** when he said: "Our self image, strongly held, essentially determines what we become."

Over the past month we have been purposely changing our own self-image and our image of the world, and in the process we have been mastering our mind and our self.

W. Clement Stone said: **"Self-suggestion makes you master of yourself."**

Keep mastering yourself throughout your life by creating your own self-image through affirmations

Day 20:

If you don't feel good, change your thoughts!

If you are doing anything and you feel bad, STOP!

Do something to get yourself feeling better.

Remember the one simple practice you can do easily from anywhere...just write your feelings, then forgive yourself. Say, "Thank you" and, "I love you," then return to your positive affirmations and vision.

That simple process gets you feeling better, and it is a lasting positive solution, unlike *stuffing your face*, or *drowning your sorrows*, or *distracting your mind*, or feeding any other physical craving.

Day 22:

Napoleon Hill once said: "One must marry one's feelings to one's beliefs and ideas. That is probably the only way to achieve a measure of harmony in one's life."

Remember how important it is to pay close attention to your feelings.   And get yourself feeling good.

If you feel good, that means you're thinking about what you want…you are thinking faithfully and you are full of belief.

If you feel bad, look at what you're thinking!

If you feel bad, that unequivocally means you are thinking thoughts of **doubt**, **fear**, or **worry** about something.

When you notice yourself feeling bad to any degree (**the sooner you notice the better**), change your thoughts.

Rhonda Byrne in **The Secret** said: "Ask once, believe you have received, and all you have to do to receive is feel good. <u>If you are feeling good, it is because you are thinking good thoughts.</u>"

You can tell if you believe by how you feel.

Living the 12 pillars of a Truly Amazing Life makes you feel good.

If you go through life feeling amazing consistently isn't that a Truly Amazing Life?

That is why these 12 pillars are so vital and why it's so valuable to keep this poster visible

(Go to **http://TrulyAmazingLife.com/ayt-resources** to download and print the poster for free)

Day 23:

"**A wise man will be master of his mind. A fool will be its slave.**" - Publilius Syrus

"O be wise...what can I say more?" - Jacob 6:12, *The Book of Mormon*

That's all for our review...and really...what can I say more on this topic? I think I've been abundantly clear and I hope it has helped you tremendously.

Keep feeling good as you *Affirm Your Truth*! That is ultimate wisdom. That is how you master your mind.

Tomorrow we'll tie it all together...

...Make today amazing!

Day 30 - Remember the importance of the 10,000 strikes.

You did it! Congratulations!

By religiously doing your affirmations for 30 days you are now a new person.

Your subconscious beliefs have been altered, whether you feel any different or not.

It is likely that your experience and enjoyment of life has already significantly improved. If not, **don't worry**, keep *Affirming Your Truth*!

If you have been feeling good each time you have done your affirmations, celebrate that! Keep doing it.

Remember the statement we began with 30 days ago?

Repetition while evoking deep emotion is a key to lasting internal change.

Let's wrap up with a final discussion on the critical importance of *repeated focus on the fundamentals.*

This is the end of the month, but just the beginning of a wonderful journey of **Affirming Your Truth** the rest of your life.

The Shao Lin monks who were the originators of Kung Fu and true mental masters were known to say:

"I am not afraid of the 10,000 strikes you have practiced once. <u>*I am deathly afraid of the ONE strike you have practiced 10,000 times.*</u>"

By practicing only the fundamental movements over and over and over, they became so skilled they could often end a confrontation completely with just one punch.

Do you want to become a master at living life?

Focus on the Fundamentals!

And what are the fundamentals of living a Truly Amazing Life?

You have been laser focused on the **most fundamental** of all the fundamentals for the last 30 days...

Believe that 'This is a Truly Amazing Life' and 'Everything is conspiring for your benefit.'

Because you have taken action with me daily for the last 30 days you have now successfully created one of the most empowering and most fundamental habits ever...

...Daily, purposeful, **emotional** directing of your thoughts.

Each day you increase your ability to **believe** with this habit to *Affirm Your Truth*

Now you should go forth and continue this habit and increase your belief each day for the rest of your life.

And what are the **other fundamentals** of a Truly Amazing Life?

The other 11 pillars:

- **Celebrate**. Play! Love your life today.

- **Enjoy** every moment.

- **Smile!** Appreciate everything.

- **Think** faithfully.

- **Create** *art. Create the life you want.*

- **Succeed** right now.

- **Remember** who you are.

- **Empower** others.

- **Give** yourself away.

- **Grow**. Expand your mind.

- **Love** unconditionally.

Those are the fundamentals.

There are eleven other four-week habit creation systems like this one — each focused on one of those fundamentals.

This is a 12 month series designed to help you improve at living each of the 12 habits of a Truly Amazing Life...one month at a time — all year long.

And when the year is over...we start back at the beginning!

The fundamentals of a Truly Amazing Life will always be the fundamentals — they don't change.

Wisdom is living like the true mental masters, the Shao Lin monks — constantly focusing on the fundamentals throughout life.

Check the epilogue at the end of this book for links to all of the other training systems in this 12-part series. And now to wrap this month up...

...**What are your next steps with the *Affirm Your Truth* habit?**

1. Keep **writing**, **affirming**, **visualizing**, and **feeling** the empowering truths you want your life to be guided by every single day.

2. Each month going forward, choose a few different beliefs to focus on and rotate them in to your key 5 to 10 affirmations short list.

3. Email me at aaron@trulyamazinglife.com and tell me your experience!

Did this 30-day system positively impact your life?

If so, how?

I want to hear from you. I read and appreciate every response I get regardless of its nature.

<u>I really appreciate hearing experiences of how this has helped you.</u>

But also, did you feel like this system could be improved in any way to be more helpful for you?

<u>If so, **how**?</u>

Please share your insights with me so I can better serve you and everyone else in the future.

And don't worry about offending me...*I can take it* ;) I really want to know how I can improve to be more helpful...

Thank you for sticking with me and mostly **thank you for taking action**!

<u>Make Today Amazing!</u>

So What's Next?

You have now completed the training on habit #1 of the 12 Habits of a Truly Amazing Life.

I hope you have given it your heart and committed yourself to the simple practices for the full month.

That is how you will gain the most value in your life from this book. If you just so happened to opt for 'Way #2' of reading this book, and you read the whole thing in a day or two…now it's time for some self-discipline!

Make sure to be diligent about going back through each day *one at a time* and <u>**take the actions over the course of an entire month!**</u>

You will never know how impactful it could have been in your life if you don't.

<u>Remember…living a Truly Amazing Life is a matter of habit.</u> If you don't take the actions, you won't get the habits.

But when you do take the actions to establish or strengthen any one of the habits of a Truly Amazing Life — life flows more smoothly.

It doesn't mean you won't experience hard things, but your ability to go through life with *poise* and *grace* dramatically improves.

Living the Truly Amazing Life habits makes you like a wise sage — freed from the burdens of **attachment to pleasures** and **aversion to pain**. You can then embrace all that is and make the best of it in a state of peace and calm.

Having the 12 habits operating in your life is like building a house with power tools instead of slaving away with a handheld screwdriver and a handsaw.

You can do so much more, with greater ease and happiness, when you have these powerful habits installed.

I invite you to build on what you have started here and stay committed to living a Truly Amazing Life <u>by focusing on another habit next month</u>.

Here's a review of the 12 Habits & The 12 Pillars of a Truly Amazing Life:

	The Pillar	The Habit	The Book
1	Believe	Affirm	Affirm Your Truth
2	Remember	Reflect	Remember Who You Are
3	Smile	Appreciate	Feel Better Faster
4	Enjoy	Move	Move Your Body
5	Think	Meditate	Change Your Thoughts
6	Succeed	Focus	Succeed Right Now
7	Give	Serve	Give Yourself Away
8	Create	Write	Create Your Life
9	Love	Forgive	Love Unconditionally
10	Celebrate	Play	Play Every Day
11	Grow	Read	Expand Your Mind
12	Empower	Listen	Empower Other People

The order you choose to focus on them is not critical. Pick whichever one jumps out at you or just go straight down the list.

To see all the books in the series currently available go to "http://The12Habits.com" in your web browser.

If, for example, you feel like you've been **_struggling to move your body_** and you feel that's an area that could really improve your life — go next to the **Move Your Body** training.

I guarantee that training system will open your eyes and heart to new ways of looking at that important daily habit.

Or if you **_feel disconnected from the true you,_** and you want to strengthen your inner connection, remember who you truly are, and see your magnificence inside more clearly...start with **Remember Who You Are**.

All of the pillars are powerful and important.

You can't go wrong and you'll want to focus on one of the 12 habits each month anyway.

You'll get through each of them in one year taking one month at a time, so don't worry about what you may be missing. _**Just make a decision and take action**_.

If the decision is hard for you — just start at the top of the list.

Here are the two foundational posters once more in case you didn't yet take the opportunity to download and print them at the beginning of the month.

I highly encourage you to use these as daily visual reminders and motivators.

<u>Positive words in your environment carry significant power.</u>

The Make Today Amazing Poster - The 12 Habits

(Go to **http://TrulyAmazingLife.com/ayt-resources** to download and print the poster for free)

The Truly Amazing Life Poster - The 12 Pillars

(Go to **http://TrulyAmazingLife.com/ayt-resources** to download and print the poster for free)

What To Expect Going Forward

As you commit yourself to deepening these habits one per month at a time, here's what you can expect:

1 - **Simplicity** - By giving yourself only one focus per month you cut out the noise and distraction and allow for amazing growth and breakthroughs.

2 - **Consistent Growth** - Committing to strengthening one of the 12 habits of a Truly Amazing Life each month of the year will help you continue to grow and keep you from forgetting, getting swept away by life, and finding yourself lost or floundering.

3 - **Transformation** - As you systematically work on establishing one habit per month, you will look back after a year and witness remarkable change in yourself. You'll experience the wonderful benefits each month — but when you stack all of it together — It is inevitable that your life will feel incredibly rich, meaningful, and fulfilled.

That's the whole point after all...

...To live a Truly Amazing Life!

And that's what living these pillars and habits means. You literally cannot be living all 12 of these habits on a daily basis and NOT be experiencing a Truly Amazing Life.

That would be impossible.

So *trust the process* and *focus on these fundamentals* each day and each month.

In Closing

I will conclude with three huge THANK YOU's!

1 - **Thank you** for taking this training!

2 - **Thank you** for committing to yourself to constantly improve & grow.

3 - **Thank you** for your desire to live a Truly Amazing Life — the world is better because of your love.

I am truly honored that you have joined me in the commitment to never settle for mediocre ever again.

I love hearing about your experiences, **both successes and challenges**. I read every email personally at aaron@trulyamazinglife.com — please don't be shy about reaching out!

If we ever meet in person I hope to give you a big hug and thank you in person for being the beautiful soul you are. That's how I see you in my mind, and in my heart.

I know that's who you are because I can feel your love and desire for goodness even as I write this and imagine you reading and reminding yourself every single day anew that **This Is A Truly Amazing Life** and **Everything Is Conspiring For Your Benefit**.

I love you. <u>Make today amazing!</u>

~ Aaron Kennard

How You Can Help!

Thank you again for taking this self-guided training course!

I really appreciate and need your feedback and input. It helps me improve and make things better for you in the future.

Please leave me a helpful review by going to **http://TrulyAmazingLife.com/ayt-reviews** in your web browser.

Reviews go a LONG way in helping spread this life-changing work to other people who could really benefit from it.

Thank you so much!

~ Aaron Kennard

www.ingramcontent.com/pod-product-compliance
Lightning Source LLC
Chambersburg PA
CBHW020034120526
44588CB00030B/253